THE CRITICAL IDIOM REISSUED

Volume 17

NATURALISM

NATURALISM

LILIAN R. FURST AND
PETER N. SKRINE

LONDON AND NEW YORK

First published in 1971 by Methuen & Co Ltd
This edition first published in 2018
by Routledge
2 Park Square, Milton Park, Abingdon, Oxon OX14 4RN
and by Routledge
711 Third Avenue, New York, NY 10017

Routledge is an imprint of the Taylor & Francis Group, an informa business

© 1971 Lilian R. Furst and Peter N. Skrine

All rights reserved. No part of this book may be reprinted or reproduced or utilised in any form or by any electronic, mechanical, or other means, now known or hereafter invented, including photocopying and recording, or in any information storage or retrieval system, without permission in writing from the publishers.

Trademark notice: Product or corporate names may be trademarks or registered trademarks, and are used only for identification and explanation without intent to infringe.

British Library Cataloguing in Publication Data
A catalogue record for this book is available from the British Library

ISBN: 978-1-138-21971-7 (Set)
ISBN: 978-1-315-26975-7 (Set) (ebk)
ISBN: 978-1-138-24277-7 (Volume 17) (hbk)
ISBN: 978-1-138-24278-4 (Volume 17) (pbk)
ISBN: 978-1-315-11549-8 (Volume 17) (ebk)

Publisher's Note
The publisher has gone to great lengths to ensure the quality of this reprint but points out that some imperfections in the original copies may be apparent.

Disclaimer
The publisher has made every effort to trace copyright holders and would welcome correspondence from those they have been unable to trace.

Naturalism / *Lilian R. Furst and Peter N. Skrine*

*First published 1971
by Methuen & Co Ltd
11 New Fetter Lane London EC4*
© *1971 Lilian R. Furst and Peter N. Skrine
Printed in Great Britain
by Cox & Wyman Ltd, Fakenham, Norfolk*

SBN 416 65500 9 Hardback
SBN 416 65670 6 Paperback

*This title is available in both hardback and paperback editions.
The paperback edition is sold subject to the
condition that it shall not, by way of trade or
otherwise, be lent, re-sold, hired out, or otherwise
circulated without the publisher's prior consent in any
form of binding or cover other than that in which it is
published and without a similar condition including this condition
being imposed on the subsequent purchaser.*

Distributed in the U.S.A.
by Barnes & Noble Inc.

Contents

	GENERAL EDITOR'S PREFACE	vi
1	THE TERM 'NATURALISM'	1
	Its usages and history	
	Its relationship to 'Realism'	
2	THE SHAPING FACTORS	10
	The effects of industrialization	
	The impact of the sciences	
	The scientific method	
3	GROUPS AND THEORIES	24
	France	
	England	
	United States of America	
	Germany	
4	THE CREATIVE WORKS	42
	The novel	
	Drama	
5	CONCLUSION	70
	BIBLIOGRAPHY	73
	INDEX	79

The section on Drama was written by Peter N. Skrine; the other sections by Lilian R. Furst.

General Editor's Preface

This volume is one of a series of short studies, each dealing with a single key item, or a group of two or three key items, in our critical vocabulary. The purpose of the series differs from that served by the standard glossaries of literary terms. Many terms are adequately defined for the needs of students by the brief entries in these glossaries, and such terms will not be the subjects of studies in the present series. But there are other terms which cannot be made familiar by means of compact definitions. Students need to grow accustomed to them through simple and straightforward but reasonably full discussions of them. The purpose of this series is to provide such discussions.

Some of the terms in question refer to literary movements (e.g., 'Romanticism', 'Aestheticism', etc.), others to literary kinds (e.g., 'Comedy', 'Epic', etc.), and still others to stylistic features (e.g., 'Irony', 'The Conceit', etc.). Because of this diversity of subject matter, no attempt has been made to impose a uniform pattern upon the studies. But all authors have tried to provide as full illustrative quotation as possible, to make reference whenever appropriate to more than one literature, and to compose their studies in such a way as to guide readers towards the short bibliographies in which they have made suggestions for further reading.

John D. Jump

University of Manchester

I
The Term 'Naturalism'

ITS USAGES AND HISTORY

Naturalism, with its twin adjectives 'naturalist' and 'naturalistic', is a deceptive term. It immediately evokes associations with 'nature' and 'naturalness' so that we tend to assume too easily and too vaguely that we know, if not its precise meaning, at least its area of reference. But the more examples of it we come across, the more we become aware of its wide range and its complex undertones. Nor is it a term of rarified scholarly criticism only. Within less than a month early in 1970 it cropped up four times in my casual reading of newspapers: Iris Murdoch's *A Fairly Honourable Defeat* was described as 'a book of ideas and images and not a naturalistic work'; Ronald Firbank was classed as 'an aesthete, not a naturalist' (a phrase that might well lead one to visualize him as a collector of paintings rather than of plants!); John Updike's *Couples* was dismissed in a German paper as a piece of 'flat naturalism', while the editor of the French *Jardin des Modes* 'admires tremendously the bold naturalism of English girls, but cannot understand the success of the bottom-skimming miniskirt'.

These random recent examples might suggest two things: that 'naturalism' occurs chiefly in literary criticism and that it is a popular term of our time. Neither of these conclusions would in fact be correct. 'Naturalism' has a very long history and it was not introduced into the literary arena until relatively late. In this respect it is similar to the term 'romantic' which also denoted an attitude before it described an artistic tendency. And just as Romantic ideas and styles existed before, and persisted after, the specifically Romantic

2 NATURALISM

period of the early nineteenth century, likewise Naturalism can be found well before and after the late nineteenth and early twentieth-century movement of that name. 'Entre la fin du Moyen-Age et la fin du XVIIIième siècle, les naturalistes sont nombreux' ('between the end of the Middle Ages and the end of the eighteenth century there were many naturalists'), including Velasquez, Caravaggio, Raphaël and Shakespeare, according to this critic (A. David-Sauvageot, *Le réalisme et le naturalisme*, Paris, 1889, p. 95); to another historian the early Naturalists were Socrates, Euripides, Virgil, Rutebeuf, Villon, Marot, Rabelais, Montaigne, Racine, Molière, Descartes, Bossuet, La Rochefoucauld, La Bruyère, La Fontaine, Charles Sorel, Fontenelle, Bayle, Marivaux, Lesage, Prévost, Laclos, Rousseau, Diderot, Rétif de la Bretonne, etc. (C. Beuchat, *Histoire du naturalisme français*, Paris, 1949, i, pp. 21–32). Elsewhere we read that Rabelais was 'a realist' who 'preached a naturalistic ethic' (H. Levin, *The Gates of Horn*, Oxford, 1966, p. 66), or that 'Diderot pushed naturalism as literal deception to astonishing extremes' (R. Wellek, *Concepts of Criticism*, New Haven, 1963, p. 224). Brandes' volume on *Naturalism in England* is about Wordsworth, Shelley, Byron and Scott, while in Germany Goethe's lyric poems have been acclaimed as 'naturalistisch'. There is no need to multiply these examples any further to show firstly, that as a term 'Naturalism' is not readily comprehensible, and secondly, that as a phenomenon it is not confined to the late nineteenth century.

Originally 'Naturalism' was used in ancient philosophy to denote materialism, epicureanism or any secularism. For long this was the primary meaning of the word. Eighteenth-century Naturalism, as elaborated by the thinker Holbach, was a philosophical system that saw man living solely in a world of perceived phenomena, a kind of cosmic machine which determined his life as it did nature, in short, a universe devoid of transcendental, metaphysical or divine forces. That this was the chief meaning of 'Naturalism' well into the nineteenth century is shown by a large number of statements as well as by the dictionary definitions of the time. Ambroise Paré, for instance, a famous sixteenth-century surgeon, regarded it as the doctrine of epicurean atheists. Diderot wrote of the Naturalists as those who do not admit God but who believe instead in material substance. Sainte-Beuve in 1839 bracketed Naturalism with materialism or pantheism as though they were quite interchangeable, and even some half a century later, in 1882, the philosopher Caro contrasted Naturalism with spiritualism. The predominance of this philosophical sense of the term is brought out by the definition in Littré's *Dictionnaire de la langue française* (1875): 'système de ceux qui attribuent tout à la nature comme premier principe' ('the system of those who find all primary causes in nature'). Here the omission is as revealing as the definition itself; Littré, compiling his dictionary in 1875, makes no mention whatsoever of any literary connotation. Current English dictionaries also still place the philosophical and theological meaning before the artistic. So even though the earliest equation of Naturalism with materialism has in the last hundred years or so been overlaid with various elaborations, this first sense of the term has by no means died out, nor is it irrelevant to an artistic movement that attached the greatest importance to the tangible objects of the visible world.

In all the older usages I have quoted the Naturalist is portrayed as a man with an overriding interest in the material substance of this world, in its natural manifestations and physical laws. From this it was a small and obvious step to the association of 'Naturalism' with 'naturalist' in the sense 'he who studies external nature'. In the early nineteenth century the Romantics' cult of naturalness and spontaneity and the poets' tremendous delight in nature gave a powerful new impetus to the study of nature. The world was conceived as a unified living organism of creatures, plants, stars and stones, all participating in the life of the universe. Fanciful though this notion may in itself seem, it indirectly fostered the nascent sciences by encouraging men actually to observe and analyse physical phenomena in an attempt to fathom their workings. With the prodigious development of the natural sciences in the early nineteenth century, notably in the work of Lamarck (1744–1829) and Cuvier (1769–1832), the terms 'naturalism' and 'naturalist' lost some of their earlier pejorative colouring of epicurean atheism and gained a new respectability from the link with serious research.

Alongside the philosophical and the scientific, and connected with them, there was another usage of the word 'naturalist': in the fine arts. From the seventeenth century onwards a naturalist painter was one who depicted not historico-mythological or allegorical subjects, but sought to give on canvas as exact an imitation as possible of the real forms of nature. In this sense the word occurred frequently in nineteenth-century art criticism, specially in France in the writings of Baudelaire and Castagnary who maintained in his *Salon de 1863* that 'L'école naturaliste affirme que l'art est l'expression de la vie sous tous ses modes et à tous ses degrés, et que son but unique est de reproduire la nature en l'amenant à son maximum de puissance et d'intensité' ('the naturalist school asserts that art is the expression of life in all its forms and degrees, and that its sole aim is to reproduce nature at the height of its force and intensity'). This ideal is clearly based on a mimetic realism ('reproduire la nature'), but there is an added ingredient in the final phrase ('en l'amenant à son maximum de puissance et d'intensité') which gives some leeway to the artist's contribution, whether in his choice of the moment of portrayal or the manner. Castagnary's text is – perhaps deliberately – imprecise, but the possibility is certainly left open. In its very ambivalence Castagnary's definition is important for, and characteristic of, Naturalism in the arts.

It was from the fine arts that the term was finally imported into literary criticism, almost certainly by Zola in the preface to the second edition of *Thérèse Raquin* (1867). In the 1860s, through his

THE TERM 'NATURALISM' 5

school-friend Cézanne, Zola had been introduced to many of the Impressionist painters and had taken up the cudgels on their behalf with his customary energy and enthusiasm. At that time the Impressionists were very much the outsiders, engaged in a bitter struggle against the artistic Establishment of the *Académie des Beaux-Arts* which favoured dark and dull historico-mythological pictures and repeatedly rejected the Impressionists' brilliantly coloured, subtle studies of the town and country scenes around them. The young painters chose everyday subjects from contemporary reality because they were interested above all in observing the changing play of colour and light. These new ideals, as well as the courage that inspired them, were immensely exciting to Zola, and although he may not fully have understood the Impressionists' intentions, he published a series of flamboyantly daring reviews of their exhibitions. In these articles Zola used the words 'impressionist', 'realist', 'actualist' and 'naturalist' freely and synonymously. There can be little doubt that this was the source of its literary currency.

ITS RELATIONSHIP TO 'REALISM'

'Naturalism' thus came on to the literary scene already loaded with meanings derived from philosophy, the sciences and the fine arts. What is more, it arrived at the hey-day of Realism and somehow in its wake. It was tied to the apron-strings of 'Realism' from its first appearance, from Zola's tacit assumption in his art criticism that the terms were virtually identical. He made no attempt at a clear distinction in his various *Salons* nor, as far as I can ascertain, in any of his subsequent literary criticism. The overlapping of 'Naturalism' with 'Realism' is indeed a great, perhaps the greatest, bug-bear of this topic.

Almost without exception critics have been in the habit of grouping the two terms together or at least of writing about both, irrespective of whether their work was supposed to be about Realism or about Naturalism. Many have even categorically expressed their conviction that 'le réalisme et le naturalisme ne sont qu'une seule et même chose' ('Realism and Naturalism are merely one and the same thing') (C. Beuchat, *Histoire du naturalisme français*, i, p. 11). Some are even more generous by throwing 'Impressionism' into the stew as well. This is the practice of Brunetière whose *Le Roman naturaliste* devotes much attention to Flaubert, George Eliot, Dickens and Tolstoy, novelists whom we should probably call realists (or romantic realists if we wanted to be precise). That Brunetière envisaged no difference between 'realistic' and 'naturalistic' becomes plain from his praise of *Madame Bovary* which is hailed in one place (p. 30) as 'le chef-d'oeuvre peut-être du roman réaliste' ('perhaps the masterpiece of the realistic novel'), while later in the same book (p. 302) Flaubert is called 'le vrai héraut du naturalisme, comme il est bien probable que *Madame Bovary* en demeurera le chef-d'oeuvre' ('the true harbinger of Naturalism, just as *Madame Bovary* will probably remain its masterpiece'). Whether *Madame Bovary* in fact belongs to Realism or to Naturalism is irrelevant at this stage; the point is that to so eminent a critic the two terms appear to have been synonymous.

It would, however, be wrong in this case to ascribe the confusion to the critics. The exponents of Naturalism were themselves guilty of a good deal of muddled thinking which is reflected in their word-usage. The fact that the acknowledged high-priest of Naturalism, Zola, made no clear distinction may well have been influential. Of his immediate disciples Huysmans constantly spoke of 'le réalisme ou le naturalisme' throughout his impassioned defence of Zola's practices in *Emile Zola et 'L'Assommoir'*. This might have been deliberate, an attempt to make Naturalism acceptable under the guise of Realism, as it undoubtedly was in the case of Zola's *La Terre* which was presented in the 1889 English edition as '*The Soil, a realistic novel*'. With Huysmans and many of his contemporaries the confusion more likely stems from a genuine inability to distinguish between the two. One of the difficulties lay, of course, in the lack of a definition of 'Realism' in the mid-nineteenth century, let alone a coherent artistic theory. Much of the writing on the subject was of an *ad hoc* nature, centred on one specific work rather than tackling the whole problem. No wonder that Arthur Morrison in an article entitled 'What is a Realist?' in the *New Review* of March 1897 complained that 'realist' was being used 'with no unanimity of intent' and 'with so loose an application' that it was not easy 'to make a guess at its real meaning'. In America in the 1890s 'Realism' and 'Naturalism' were applied with disconcerting looseness, and Garland's term 'Veritism' (perhaps indebted to the Italian *verismo*) merely added to the unmerry fray. As for Germany here are the synonyms for 'Naturalism' listed by Leo Berg in *Der Naturalismus* (1892): 'Natürlichkeit', 'Naturerkenntnis', 'Naturkraft', 'Natursinn', 'Naturgefühl', 'Naturwahrheit', 'Naturgemässheit', 'Naturempfindung', 'Rückkehr zur Natur', 'Annäherung an die Natur', 'Liebe zur Natur', 'Naturfreiheit', 'Natureinfachheit', 'Natureinheit', 'Naturschönheit', 'Naturwirklichkeit', 'Naturwissenschaft', 'Naturfreude', 'Kampf gegen Unnatur'. It is a list which in its subtlety as well as its monotony defies translation, but it gives support to the suggestion made as long ago as 1884 by Desprez in *L'Évolution naturaliste* that one could with the term 'Naturalism' rival Musset's brilliant satire on the meanings and interpretations of 'Romanticism' in *Les Lettres de Dupuis et Cotonet*. More soberly, the present situation is well summarized by Becker in his introduction to *Documents of Modern Literary Realism*:

> Though the words *realism* and *naturalism* are freely, even rashly, used, there is no general agreement as to what they mean. For many they have come to be merely convenient pejoratives, especially when qualified as *stark, raw, unimaginative, superficial, atheistic*, and more recently *socialist*. (p. 3)

Is it then just part of our modern urge for greater linguistic precision that we should seek to differentiate between the two terms that have for long co-existed, even if not very happily? Or is 'Naturalism' radically separate from 'Realism'? Paradoxically, the answer to both these questions would seem to be: no. Naturalism *does* differ from Realism but is not independent of it. The most appropriate image to convey the relationship might be that of Siamese twins, who have separate limbs while sharing certain organs. What the Realists and the Naturalists have in common is the fundamental belief that art is in essence a mimetic, objective representation of outer reality (in contrast to the imaginative, subjective transfiguration practised by the Romantics). This led them to choose for their subject matter the ordinary, the close-to-hand, and also to extol the ideal of impersonality in technique. In this sense, as Harry Levin has pointed out in *The Gates of Horn*, Realism is 'a general tendency' in so far as every work of art 'is realistic in some respects and unrealistic in others' (pp. 64–5). It was out of this general tendency to mimetic Realism that Naturalism grew. In many ways it was an intensification of Realism; as L. Deffoux has fittingly put it (*Le Naturalisme*, Paris, 1929, p. 9), Realism is like the 1789 Revolution in literature while Naturalism corresponds to the 1793 Reign of Terror. But it was not just a matter of choosing more shocking subjects, earthier vocabulary, more striking slogans or more photographic details. The true difference lies much deeper: at its core is the imposition of a certain, very specific view of man on Realism's attitude of detached neutrality. Thus the Naturalists not only elaborated on and intensified the basic tendencies of Realism; they also added important new elements which turned Naturalism into a recognizable doctrine such as Realism had never been. Naturalism is therefore more concrete and at the same time more limited than Realism; it is a literary movement with distinct theories, groups and practices. Being a school and a method, Naturalism is in fact what Realism is not; on the other hand, this very demarcation in itself makes Naturalism something of lesser import than Realism which is one of the underlying tendencies of most art.

What then were these new elements that were added to mimetic Realism to produce Naturalism? They were, as we shall see, derived largely from the natural sciences; indeed one of the briefest, though necessarily incomplete, definitions of Naturalism is as an attempt to apply to literature the discoveries and methods of nineteenth-century science. This affinity to science was explicitly emphasized by the Naturalists; it becomes clear from the definition offered by Paul Alexis, Zola's closest ally, who summed up Naturalism as:

Une méthode de penser, de voir, de réfléchir, d'étudier, d'expérimenter, un besoin d'analyser pour savoir, mais non une façon spéciale d'écrire.

(A way of thinking, of seeing, of reflecting, of studying, of making experiments, a need to analyse in order to know, rather than a particular style of writing.)
(J. Huret, *Enquête sur l'évolution littéraire*, Paris, 1891, p. 189)

From the sciences then, by way of a philosophy itself deeply imbued with scientific thought, the Naturalists took a definite concept of man which they aimed to express in their writings. Their biological and philosophical assumptions separate them from the Realists with their unbiased objectivity, for in observing life the Naturalists already expect a certain pattern. In order to understand their views and methods we must at this stage look at the scientific and philosophic trends of the mid-nineteenth century which were so decisive in shaping this movement.

2
The Shaping Factors

The nineteenth century was a period of rapid and radical change. The entire face of Western Europe and North America was transformed under the onslaught of the Industrial Revolution. The scientific discoveries of the age forced man to a total re-assessment of his view of himself both as a physical and as a moral being. Never before had man's environment, his image of himself, his attitude to himself altered so deeply in so relatively short a span of time. And this upheaval coincided also with a whole series of political convulsions that punctuated the nineteenth century: the revolutions of 1830 and 1848, Louis-Napoleon's *coup d'état* of 1851, the unification of Germany and of Italy, the Franco-Prussian war, the American Civil War, etc. It is obviously impossible within the space of this monograph to give more than the briefest sketch of these changes. But however scant the details, let there be no doubt as to the importance of these developments for Naturalism: the social, scientific, philosophical and ethical trends of the nineteenth century are not just the background to Naturalism; they are the crucial shaping factors that gave the movement its content, its method, its direction and even its mood.

THE EFFECTS OF INDUSTRIALIZATION

By the second quarter of the nineteenth century the effects of the Industrial Revolution were already manifest. The facts about the innovations at this period can easily be gathered from any textbook of economic history: the growth of towns, the establishment of factories, the opening of new sources of power in gas and electricity, the harnessing of steam in Nasmyth's steam hammer (1842) and the first steam-locomotive railway lines between Stockton and Darlington in 1825. This was a time of expansion and of excitement as well as of grimy slums and shocking exploitation of human and mineral resources. The Industrial Revolution is full of these sharp contrasts. On the one hand, man seemed to be conquering his world, reaping its riches (gold was discovered in California in 1848, and in Australia in 1851, and oil in the U.S.A. in 1859), establishing new forms of communication (Morse telegraph was introduced in 1837, regular steamship services to America in 1838, the penny postage in 1840; a submarine cable was laid between Dover and Calais in 1851, and the following year saw the first airship flight by Giffard). With such staggering progress no wonder that prosperity and happiness appeared to be within man's reach – or at least within the reach of some men. For this upsurge had its reverse side in the misery of the masses, the human fodder of the industrial machine. The proud catalogue of advance is partnered by the grim one of social unrest: the Luddite shattering of machines in England in 1811–15, the revolts of the silk-weavers in Lyons in 1831 and 1834, the weavers' riots in Silesia and Bohemia in 1844. The improvements that were gradually made only serve to underline how ghastly conditions had been: the Anti-combination laws were repealed in England in 1824 and the Chartist movement founded in 1836; 1841 brought the first law for the protection of workmen in France; in 1842 Ashley's Act forbade child or female labour underground and it was followed up in Graham's Factory Act of 1844 regulating the working hours of women and children, which were reduced to ten a day in 1848 in the English textile industry. Workers began to unite: in a Co-operative Society in England in 1843, in a trade union in Germany in 1844 and the Labour Association formed in Berlin in 1848, the year of the Communist Manifesto and of Louis Blanc's *Droit au travail* (*The Right to Work*).

Both these aspects of the Industrial Revolution feature in the works of the Naturalists. The scramble for money and power through commercial expansion is the explicit theme of Zola's *L'Argent*, Dreiser's *The Financier*, and *The Octopus* and *The Pit* by Norris, to name only a few. The plight of the workers, driven to strike and revolt, is best illustrated in Zola's *Germinal* and Hauptmann's *Die Weber*. Occasionally, as for instance in Zola's *Au Bonheur des dames* and Bennett's *Clayhanger*, the increasing prosperity of the owning group is portrayed alongside the desperate struggle of the have-nots. Such subjects in themselves, with their evident class consciousness, were relatively new in literature. They show how the Naturalists expanded the thematic and particularly the social range of the arts by dealing with a greater variety of people and problems, including many drawn from the newly emergent urban working classes. In this respect the Naturalists are directly linked to the Industrial Revolution and its aftermath.

Besides these obvious surface transformations, there were also other subtler and perhaps deeper consequences of industrialization. Because of their very subtlety and depth it is difficult to pinpoint them precisely. I am referring to changes of attitude and ideal, about which it is always dangerous to generalize. In 1867 Walter Bagehot commented in *The English Constitution* on the growth of 'a certain matter-of-factness' which he attributed primarily to the spread of business with its emphasis on material fruits, profit and the '"stock-taking" habit'. Bagehot called this worship of visible value, of the concrete tangible result, 'literalness'. Whatever its name, there can be no question of the existence of this trend and of its importance in the late nineteenth century. In origin it may well be almost as much a reaction against the Romantics' excessive idealism as a response to the Industrial Revolution. As to its effects there can be no doubt: it brought about a change in the dominant scale of values. With their growing awareness of the physical world men came to prize more and more its material fabric and to concentrate on externals, goods, things. That John Stuart Mill's Utilitarianism was formulated at this time was no accident.

These changes were bound to impinge on spiritual life. It is worth recalling at this point that 'Realism' is derived from *res*, the Latin word for 'thing', and that 'Naturalism' used to be tantamount to 'materialism'. Naturalism is clearly in consonance with the mood of the age which it reflects in its overwhelming emphasis on facts. The Naturalists believed that the truthfulness for which they aimed could be gained only from a painstaking observation of reality and a careful notation of fact. There are many, sometimes comical, stories of their journeys through the world notebook in hand – Zola riding (trembling) on a railway engine for *La Bête humaine*, going down a mine for *Germinal*, measuring the dimensions of a prostitute's room for *Nana*, or Moore in search of background for *A Mummer's Wife* travelling to Hanley because it had been recommended to him as the ugliest town in Britain. To some extent – and the exact extent is debatable – the Naturalists were inspired by the new art of photography which had been invented by Saint-Victor in 1824 and developed in 1839 by Daguerre. To all of them can be applied the Goncourts' phrase from *Charles Demailly*: 'je suis un homme pour qui le monde visible existe' ('I am a man for whom the visible world exists'), which is complemented by Wilhelm Bölsche's proclamation: 'das Metaphysische muss uns fern bleiben' ('the metaphysical must be kept away') (reprinted in E. Ruprecht, *Literarische Manifeste des Naturalismus*, p. 96). So the Naturalists fastened on to the object which they sought to describe with the precision of delineated detail instead of the characteristically Romantic practice of evoking sensations through the blurred contours of a musical expression. Convinced, as E. Goncourt put it in the preface to *Les Frères Zemganno*, that 'seuls, disons-le bien haut, les documents humains font les bons livres' ('only human documents make good books, let's say it loud and clear') the Naturalists subjected to a microscopic analysis the facts they had gathered. In this belief and in this method their art was in keeping with major trends of their age. For if the materialism consequent to industrialization led to a premium on factuality, this was re-inforced a hundredfold by the impact of the sciences.

THE IMPACT OF THE SCIENCES

It is hard for us fully to grasp the impact of the sciences in the mid-nineteenth century, nor is this the place to go into it. With the enormous number of discoveries in the past hundred years, indeed in our life-time, we have tended to become blasé. Perhaps this is due also to the technical complexity of recent achievements, whose mathematical, computerized intricacies are way beyond average comprehension. We watch with astonishment the antics of the first men on the moon on our television screens, but we hardly consider them of immediate or direct relevance to our own daily lives. We joke about the prospect of a fortnight's package-tour to the moon – because we don't seriously envisage the possibility. The situation was very different in the mid-nineteenth century. To begin with, the scientific discoveries were technically less sophisticated; some understanding of their outlines was more likely for the ordinary educated person, specially as there was not yet the separation of the two cultures that bedevils our century. So there was more of a general intelligent interest in science, more of an endeavour to follow its findings than nowadays. What is more, many of the discoveries had a prompt practical application, such as the use of steam-power or gas; they transformed the face of the earth in their industrial development and probably helped to make people aware of their personal involvement in scientific advances. Such advances had also more novelty appeal

THE SHAPING FACTORS 15

then than now. Finally, men's attitude to the idea of a changing universe had not the flexibility, the easy passive acceptance with which we today are prepared to swallow, and to adjust to, unpalatable truths. The mid-nineteenth century man felt much more sure of himself and at home in his world; he was therefore more liable to be shocked than we are, and more ready to resist if need be.

Progress in the sciences during the nineteenth century was so manifold that not even the most potted of surveys can be attempted here; that must be left to the historians of science. Suffice it to say that in every single field – physics, chemistry, biology, medicine – the advances were fundamental in character and inestimably far-reaching in their implications. In so far as one area can be singled out, it must be the biological sciences, both for the startling nature of the discoveries and for their direct relevance to thought and literature. Quite early in the century Lamarck had already gone a long way towards the theory of evolution which posits that plants and animals develop by gradual modification from previously existing forms of life. With the publication in 1859 of Darwin's *Origin of Species by means of Natural Selection* the theory of evolution became the most controversial topic of the age. Darwin maintained that man is descended from the lower animals and that in animal life there is a continuous struggle for existence which leads to the survival of the fittest by a process of natural selection. The very suggestion, further elaborated in *The Descent of Man* (1871), that man was closely related to apes was in itself profoundly shocking, indeed personally insulting to the Victorians' self-possession. As for the notion of natural selection, the belief that the strong survived while the weak went under, this ran counter to all religious teaching and was inevitably anathema to genteel morality. The furore aroused by the *Origin of Species* is therefore hardly surprising; it was the centre of a virulent controversy which need not be re-told here. As so often happens, however, far from suppressing the object of attack, the opposition merely provided more publicity. In 1860 the *Origin of Species* was translated into German, and into French in 1862. Its influence spread rapidly in ever-widening circles, and in retrospect it is no exaggeration to call it *the* crucial landmark of nineteenth-century science and thought. Whether they wished or not, men were forced into the most radical self-reassessment in human history. Instead of being creatures of the Divine Will, they had to accept themselves as only slightly above the animal level, and life itself as a continuous struggle—a bitter and chunky pill to swallow, let alone to digest.

In the development of Naturalism Darwin's theory is without doubt the most important single shaping factor. The Naturalists' view of man is directly dependent on the Darwinian picture of his descent from the lower animal. In contrast to the idealization of man by the Romantics, the Naturalists deliberately reduce him to animal level, stripping him of higher aspirations. 'L'homme métaphysique' was being replaced by 'l'homme physiologique' according to Zola (*Une Campagne* (1880–1), Charpentier, Paris, 1913, p. 129), the title of one of whose novels, *La Bête humaine* (*The Human Animal*) could serve as a descriptive tag to many naturalistic figures. The Naturalists even seem to reverse the process of evolution by showing the degeneration of man into a sub-human state, as in Norris' *Vandover and the Brute*, Zola's *L'Assommoir* and Hauptmann's *Vor Sonnenaufgang*. Particularly in a crisis, under some stress or the impetus of the sexual urge or the influence of alcohol, man (as Freud was to show a little later) reverts to the primitive brutalism latent within himself. The recurrent imagery of naturalist writing is drawn from the animal world, and its vocabulary, as M. Cowley has pointed out in his 'Natural History of American Naturalism', abounds in the 'law of claw and fang', 'primordial', 'struggle for existence', 'savage', 'driving', 'con-

THE SHAPING FACTORS 17

quering', 'cyclopean', 'abyss', 'the blood of his Viking ancestors' and so forth. Needless to say, this conception of man aroused much resentment and laid the Naturalists open to attack from many quarters.

The Naturalists' Darwinian view of man was supported by factors from various other sources, themselves often indebted to Darwin. One example of this is the theory of heredity, which is in a sense a variant on evolution within the human realm. A firm conviction of the cardinal role of heredity is common to nearly all the Naturalists. Zola was deeply impressed by his reading in 1868–9 of Dr. Prosper Lucas' *Traité philosophique et physiologique de l'hérédité naturelle dans les états de santé et de maladie du système nerveux, avec l'application méthodique des lois de la procréation au traitement général des affections dont elle est le principe* (*Philosophical and physiological treatise on natural heredity in the healthy and the diseased nervous system, together with the consistent application of the laws of procreation to the general treatment of the states engendered by it*). Zola's conception of the *Rougon-Macquart* series as the 'natural and social history of a family' is patently inspired by the doctrine of heredity, strong traces of which are found throughout naturalist writing. Heredity, in the guise of innate urges and instincts, was also one of the three main principles of Hippolyte Taine (1828–93), whose function was virtually that of go-between between science and literature. In the preface to the second edition of his *Essais de critique et d'histoire* (1866) he popularized Darwin's ideas. 'L'animal humain continue l'animal brut' ('the human animal is a continuation of the primitive animal'); in both 'la molécule originelle est héréditaire et la forme acquise se transmet en partie et lentement par l'hérédité' ('the primary molecule is inherited, and its acquired shape is passed on partially and gradually by heredity'); in both 'la molécule organisée ne se développe que sous l'influence du milieu' ('the molecule as it is develops only under the influence of its environment') (H. Taine, *Essais de critique et d'histoire*,

18 NATURALISM

Paris, 1920, p. xxviii). To these purely biological factors Taine adds 'le moment', immediate circumstances, to complete the explanation of human behaviour.

So to the Naturalists man is an animal whose course is determined by his heredity, by the effect of his environment and by the pressures of the moment. This terribly depressing conception robs man of all free will, all responsibility for his actions, which are merely the inescapable result of physical forces and conditions totally beyond his control. As R. Chase has said, 'Naturalistic doctrine assumes that fate is sometimes imposed on the individual from the outside. The protagonist of a naturalistic novel is therefore at the mercy of circumstances rather than of himself, indeed he often seems to *have* no self' (R. Chase, *The American Novel and its Tradition*, London, 1957, p. 199). Consequently Naturalism tends to present 'case histories rather than tragedies in the classical sense' (M. Cowley, 'A Natural History of American Naturalism', in G. Becker, *Documents of Modern Literary Realism*, p. 449). This is a serious criticism that pinpoints one of the chief weaknesses of Naturalism as a literary movement. Its conception of man is so narrow – and so tendentious – as to form a straitjacket. The writer in fact has no more liberty than his characters. The abundance of outer concrete detail is no compensation for the psychological simplification.

THE SCIENTIFIC METHOD

The methods of the sciences were adopted with as much alacrity as their matter. With its emphasis on a rational analysis of observed data the scientific method was bound to appeal to the matter-of-fact mentality of the age. It was readily applied to philosophy, theology, psychology and literature, all of which were thereby interconnected in a recognizably mid-nineteenth century style of thought and approach.

In philosophy the scientific method bred Positivism, expounded by Auguste Comte in a series of works published between 1830 and his death in 1857. Applying the idea of evolution (already familiar in France through the work of Lamarck) to human thought, Comte envisaged its progress towards maturity in three stages: the theological, which produced mythical thinking, was succeeded by the abstractions of the metaphysical period and triumphantly capped by the 'positive' thought of the scientific era. Philosophical positivism is thus a system stemming from the acceptance of the scientific method as the sole means of attaining valid knowledge. Like the scientist, we can only know what we can observe or logically deduce from our observations, Comte maintained; but because all phenomena are related in a chain of cause and effect, we can draw certain conclusions in this determined world. The parallelism with the sciences is perfectly plain; positivism is in fact an attempt to subject philosophy to the scientific method and to understand the universe in scientific terms. As Comte defined it in his *Cours de philosophie positive* (2nd edition, Paris, 1864, i, p. 16), 'La caractère fondamentale de la philosophie positive est de regarder tous les phénomènes comme assujettis à des *lois* naturelles invariables, dont la découverte précise et la réduction au moindre nombre possible sont le but de tous nos efforts' ('The basis of positive philosophy is to see all phenomena as subject to constant natural *laws*, and its aim is the exact discovery and schematization of these laws'). As is apparent from this definition, Positivism offered a prototype approach rather than a new doctrine. Its real significance for the nineteenth century and after lay in its methodology, its transference of the scientific into hitherto speculative domains, and this accounts for its role in the study of religion and later in the development of sociology.

Herbert Spencer (1820–1903) ought also to be mentioned in this context. His ideas, set forth in five major works, caused much excitement in the nineteenth century, specially in England and the U.S.A. Like Comte, Spencer based his philosophy on evolutionism. He regarded all development as a process of change from homogeneity to heterogeneity and he applied this principle to psychology, sociology and ethics as well as to biology. Here again we see the spread of scientific thinking into fields far beyond any narrow specialization.

The introduction of the scientific method put traditional religion under an even severer strain than Darwinism had done. In the so-called 'higher criticism' the analytical methods of modern scholarship were applied to the Bible; instead of being sacrosant as infallible holy writings, every detail was now minutely dissected. In 1849 Renan, in *L'Avenir de la science* (*The Future of Science*), claimed that the true world was far superior to fantasies of the Creation. He went on to deny miracle or mystery of any kind in his rationalistic biography of Jesus in 1863.

When the scientific method is applied to the study of man, it is equally startling. Man becomes an object to be observed, described and analysed in total neutrality; his behaviour can be understood like the workings of a machine, and it is as little subject to moral judgement as the machine because it is similarly determined (by heredity, milieu and 'moment'). Taine in fact called men 'une machine de rouages ordonnés' ('a machine with an interacting mechanism of wheels') in the preface to his *Histoire de la littérature anglaise* which contains also that famous, controversial statement that 'le vice et la vertu sont des produits comme le vitriol et le sucre' ('vice and virtue are products like vitriol and sugar'). Just as the machine that produces vitriol is not intrinsically better or worse than that which makes sugar, so the evil man is on the same plane as the good: neither is responsible for what he is, both have been conditioned by forces beyond their control. Here in essence is that amorality for which the Naturalists soon became notorious. It stems from an extension into the moral sphere of the scientific method of the age: from the belief – as Taine put it in the preface to the second edition of the *Essais de critique et d'histoire* – that the historian of human life and the scientific observer of natural phenomena have parallel tasks and therefore use parallel methods.

What is more, the creative writer too was to do exactly the same: to observe and to record as dispassionately and impersonally as the scientist. The most common analogy was that between the writer and the doctor, dissecting the human mind and body. Once again an impetus came from Taine who referred to Stendhal and Balzac as anatomists and physicians. But it was Claude Bernard's *Introduction à l'étude de la médecine expérimentale* (*Introduction to the Scientific Study of Medicine*) which was to be decisive in this context. As its title implies, it aims to transmute medicine from the intuitive art it had been into a scientific discipline dependent only on observation and deduction. Soon after its publication in 1865 it was read by Zola on whom it made such an impression that he eventually based his own *Le Roman expérimental* on it. Zola readily acknowledged his debt to Bernard, saying that the method Bernard had outlined for medicine was ideal for literature too and that he had needed merely to substitute the word 'novelist' for 'doctor'. Nowhere is there a plainer statement of the analogy between the writer and the scientist. Like the chemist, the biologist or the physicist, the artist is to 'experiment' with his material – hence the name 'roman expérimental', a name that was to prove highly misleading, in part at least because the French term 'expérience' can mean either 'experiment' or 'experience'. But this is, of course, not the only difficulty inherent in the Naturalists' attempted equation between science and literature. A good many critics would subscribe to McDowall's curt condemnation of 'the naturalistic fallacy', namely, the confusion of art with science. He defines Naturalism as 'the school of literature which holds that art should be governed by scientific method, because its human subject-matter can be measured and analysed in just the same way as the materials of the physical sciences' (A. McDowall, *Realism*, London, 1918, pp. 152–3). As a definition this is over-simplified and one-sided; a more judicious assessment is implicit in Martino's phrase (*Le Naturalisme français*, p. 217): 'une courte période d'enthousiasme exagéré, et quelquefois naïf, des hommes de lettres pour la science' ('a short phase of excessive and at times naïve enthusiasm for science on the part of men of letters'). But however much critical opinion may vary in evaluating the role of science in Naturalism as a fallacy or as an exploration of new ground, on one point there is agreement: that the scientific discoveries of the nineteenth century and the introduction of the scientific method in the arts were fundamental factors in shaping Naturalism.

Naturalism thus arose in response to the stimuli of the age which it reflected in its matter as in its manner. Essentially scientific and rational in character, it was anti-aesthetic and anti-romantic. Indeed its aims and its general tendencies have – not unjustly – often been attacked as utterly non-aesthetic, even inimical to the arts. In actual fact Naturalism was never as rational or as logically consistent as it may at first seem. The second half of the nineteenth century was a time of bewildering contradictions, of which Naturalism had its fair share. It was, as we shall see, torn between its theory and its practice, between materialism and idealism, between pessimism and optimism. On the one hand it faced the iniquities of a rapidly industrialized (polluted) world while on the other it placed boundless faith in the future progress of that world with the help of scientific advance. The Naturalists did not go as far as the Marxists in reviling the present and nurturing Messianic hopes for the future, but they did try to combine high-minded idealism with the sobriety of detached observers. Looking at the world and at man, they despaired and hoped at one and the same time. This underlying dualism helps to account for some of the apparent inconsistencies within Naturalism and it also invests the movement with a certain dialectical tension. In this respect too Naturalism is as much an expression of its age as the socio-political system of Marx and the philosophy of Nietzsche. Each represents an attempt to make a reckoning with a drastically changed universe.

3
Groups and Theories

The adherents to Naturalism tended to congregate in groups, to publish manifestos and to proclaim their artistic theories. The slogans served as a rallying-point and gave to Naturalism a strong sense of its existence as a movement. It was not, however, a single, unified movement with a clear-cut outline, as has sometimes been suggested. Three facts militate against this view: first, the groupings within each country gathered and dispersed again with considerable rapidity so that there was a constant dynamic process of development as individuals pledged their allegiance to Naturalism and later moved away. The names of Huysmans, Maupassant, Hauptmann, George Moore spring to mind immediately in this context; for them and for many other lesser writers Naturalism was one phase of their development – so much so that it is hard to find a major figure who remained a wholehearted Naturalist. (The reasons for this will be explored later in the analysis of the actual works.) Secondly, Naturalism, even in its specific literary sense and leaving aside its earlier philosophical connotations, is not limited to any well-defined time. In France it was at its height in the 1870s and early 1880s; in Germany and Italy it came a good decade later; in England it straggles from the 1890s into the opening years of this century, while in America, where its time-span is greatest, a vigorous Naturalism is in evidence between the two World Wars. So Naturalism is bounded at one end by Zola's *Thérèse Raquin* of 1867 and at the other by Steinbeck's *Grapes of Wrath* of 1939, although these dates too are subject to contention. Whatever precise dates are chosen, the fact remains that Naturalism (again like Romanticism) manifested itself in different countries at different times. What is more – and this is the third argument against its overall unity – it assumed a somewhat different guise in each land and emphasized differing aims, largely in response to native conditions and against the background of the indigenous tradition. There are, of course, fundamental common factors: the objective portrayal of closely observed reality, the adoption of the scientific method, the belief in determinism. But within this framework the variations are sufficiently great to warrant a brief survey of the dominant groups and theories of each country as a prelude to a consideration of the works produced by the Naturalists.

FRANCE

France was the fountain-head of Naturalism. This is not surprising as France had (together with England) been the home of Realism for much of the nineteenth century so that there was a logical continuity of tradition. The French Naturalists envisaged themselves as a second generation of Realists, an image that has since been repeated by many critics. In Balzac, Flaubert and, to a lesser extent, Stendhal, the Naturalists hailed the forerunners of their own school. They never tired of acclaiming these masters of the Realistic novel as their ancestors and their models. Taine's essay on Balzac in the *Nouveaux essais de critique et d'histoire* was extremely influential, and so was his appraisal of Stendhal as a 'naturaliste' and 'physicien' (H. Taine, *Histoire de la littérature anglaise*, Paris, 1877, i, p. xlvi). Huysmans paid tribute to Balzac as 'le véritable chef de notre école' ('the real leader of our school') and saw Flaubert as one of Zola's 'confrères en naturalisme' ('brothers in Naturalism') (J.-K. Huysmans, *Emile Zola et l'Assommoir*, ii, pp. 159 and 178). Zola himself, in *Les Romanciers naturalistes* (1881), wrote perceptive essays on Balzac, Stendhal and Flaubert, emphasizing those aspects of their writing whereby they could be fitted into the Naturalist pattern. The brothers

Goncourt too are often cited among the immediate precursors of Naturalism. They were close to the Naturalists in some respects, notably in their choice of commonplace subject-matter, their stress on heredity and environment as conditioning factors and their ideal of studying people 'comme un médecin, comme un savant, comme un historien' ('like a doctor, a scholar, a historian') (E. de Goncourt, *La Fille Elisa*, Paris, 1906, p. vi); but they approached the commonplace as though it were something exotic (as indeed it was to them) and they took a sensuous delight in catching ephemeral moods and scenes in luscious words so that their relevance to Naturalism is probably less than is generally assumed. Be that as it may, Realism was well established in France in the nineteenth century, and it was on the shoulders of this tradition – to borrow Auerbach's apt phrase – that the Naturalists stood (E. Auerbach, *Mimesis*, New York, 1957, p. 447).

Just as France was supreme as the source of Naturalism, so within French Naturalism – and eventually far beyond – the decisive mind was that of Emile Zola (1840–1902). His dominance over Naturalism is perhaps without parallel in the leadership of any artistic movement. As Hemmings has pointed out in an article in *French Studies* (no. 8, 1954, p. 109), as early as 1891 in Huret's *Enquête sur l'évolution littéraire*, many of the literary celebrities interviewed simply identified Naturalism with Zola. Partly this was due to the sheer force of Zola's personality; he had in his youth worked as a journalist and in the publicity department of a large publishing firm and he brought to his artistic campaigns his knowledge of these fields as well as a real innate flair for the striking expression. More important, he had the courage to speak his mind, however unpopular or unconventional his opinions were, as is shown by his championship first of the Impressionist painters and later in his life of Dreyfus. He preached the gospel of Naturalism with missionary fervour and with the extra zeal of the convert, for his earliest stories, the *Contes à Ninon* (1864) and *La*

Confession de Claude (1865), had been in the wake of an effete Romanticism.

Zola's dominance over the French Naturalists is even physically manifest in the name given to the school: *Le Groupe de Médan*, Médan being the small town not far from Paris where Zola had bought a house. In fact the group met not at Médan but at Zola's home in Paris where he regularly received on Thursdays. By the latter half of the 1870s the group had crystallized; its members were Paul Alexis (1847–1901), Henry Céard (1851–1924), Léon Hennique (1851–1935), Joris-Karl Huysmans (1848–1907) and Guy de Maupassant (1850–1893). To show their solidarity they published in 1880 *Les Soirées de Médan* to which each of the six contributed a short story. The stories had a common theme – the Franco-Prussian war of 1870 – and in the preface they claimed to 'procéder d'une idée unique, avoir une même philosophie' ('stem from a single ideal, share the same philosophy') although this philosophy is not specified other than by Maupassant's explanation in *Le Gaulois* of 17 April 1880 that *Les Soirées de Médan* were against 'la sentimentalité ronflante des romantiques' ('the Romantics' snivelling sentimentality'). There is indeed a certain harsh realism in all the stories but they are hardly of any importance as far as Naturalism goes. Except for Maupassant's *Boule de Suif*, none of the stories is of intrinsic worth. This points to the chief weakness of the Médan group: apart from Maupassant and Huysmans, none had great literary talent, and even Maupassant and Huysmans fell far short of Zola's creative power. The Médan group deserved the derisive nickname it was given in the press: 'Zola's tail'. The works of Alexis, Céard and Hennique have largely been forgotten; even their best novels (Céard's *Une Belle journée*, 1881, and Hennique's *L'Accident de Monsieur Hébert*, 1883) are rarities in any library. Nor did the Médan group make any substantial contribution to the theory of Naturalism. Maupassant's 'Le Roman', published in 1887 as a preface to *Pierre et Jean*, expounds a

Realistic rather than a Naturalistic conception of the novel, while Huysman's *Emile Zola et l'Assommoir*, which appeared in 1876 in the journal *L'Actualité*, is no more than an echo of Zola's ideas.

Almost the entire body of Naturalistic literary theory in France comes therefore from Zola. Spanning some thirty years, it comprises the 1867 preface to the second edition of *Thérèse Raquin*, *Le Roman expérimental* (1879), *Le Naturalisme au théâtre* and *Les Romanciers naturalistes* both of 1881, and finally the 1897 *Lettre à la jeunesse*. There was little or no development in Zola's views over the years so that in the *Lettre à la jeunesse* he merely reiterated the same tenets as he had laid down earlier. In many ways the preface to the second edition of *Thérèse Raquin* offers the best introduction to Zola's theories, not least because it is short and succinct. Like his other major statement of principle, *Le Roman expérimental*, the preface to *Thérèse Raquin* was written partly in self-defence to counter not just adverse criticism, but a widespread failure to understand his aims and methods.

Zola was particularly irked by the charges of immorality, to which he replied with the claim that his novel was a scientific study and that 'le reproche d'immoralité, en matière de science, ne prouve absolument rien' ('the reproach of immorality is irrelevant in the sciences'). This was to become a stock-in-trade of the Naturalists: that in their capacity as scientists they were beyond criteria of morality in matter or manner; they were neutral analysts of observed facts. The argument advanced to refute the allegation of immorality already reveals the main line of the preface to *Thérèse Raquin*, namely Zola's declaration of his scientific approach: 'mon but a été un but scientifique avant tout' ('my aim was above all a scientific one'). Throughout the preface Zola hammers this point home. Using what he calls 'la méthode moderne', working 'comme un médecin' ('like a doctor'), 'avec la seule curiosité du savant' ('with a purely scholarly interest'), he has engaged in 'l'analyse scientifique', 'l'étude d'un cas curieux de physiologie' ('the study of a strange physiological case') to produce 'pièces d'anatomie nues et vivantes' ('bare, live anatomical specimens'). This surgical attitude – the comparison is Zola's – goes hand-in-hand with a certain view of his figures: since their humanity has gone and 'l'âme est parfaitement absente' ('the soul is totally absent'), they are 'des brutes humains', ('human animals'), 'dominés par leurs nerfs et leur sang, dépourvus de libre arbitre' ('dominated by their nerves and their blood, devoid of free will'), 'des tempéraments et non des caractères' ('temperaments, not characters'), whose remorse is 'un simple désordre organique' ('merely an organic disorder'). Zola's argument hangs together reasonably well and its intent is clear enough. Whether it means very much is another matter: phrases such as 'des tempéraments et non des caractères' or 'l'âme est parfaitement absente' make excellent slogans but hardly stand up to examination. As for this theory's artistic feasibility in practice, that indeed is debatable, and we shall have to consider it more fully when we look at the works of Naturalism.

Le Roman expérimental, written when the *Rougon-Macquart* series was well under way, repeats most of the notions formulated in the preface to *Thérèse Raquin*. Where previously Zola had been justifying his own practice in one particular novel, now he is laying down the law for all writers. Brunetière's criticism of this treatise (*Le Roman naturaliste*, p. 58), that it says 'peu de choses en beaucoup de mots' ('very little in a great many words') is justified. Citing Claude Bernard's *Introduction à l'étude de la médecine expérimentale* as his model, Zola dwells again and again on 'l'idée d'une littérature déterminée par la science' ('the concept of a literature shaped by science'). Here in fact are found the classical formulae of Naturalistic literary theory:

Le roman expérimental est une conséquence de l'évolution scientifique du siècle; il continue et complète la physiologie . . .; il substitue à l'étude de l'homme abstrait, de l'homme métaphysique, l'étude de l'homme naturel, soumis aux lois physico-chimiques et déterminé par les influences du milieu;

(The experimental novel arises out of the scientific advance of our century; it is a continuation and a completion of physiology . . .; the study of abstract, metaphysical man is replaced by the study of natural man, subject to physico-chemical laws and determined by the effects of his milieu;)

The scientific analogy is the key idea. From it follows the need for absolute objectivity on the writer's part and hence the overriding importance of his method, which must be as close as possible to the scientist's analysis of his material. In both *Le Roman expérimental* and *Le Naturalisme au théâtre*, which expounds the same doctrine with reference to drama, Zola concedes his disregard for form which seemed of little import to him.

This neglect of form in favour of a primacy of matter and method was to have serious consequences for Naturalist writing. It is, of course, only one weakness of a doctrine that has, and rightly, been attacked from all sides. Critics have been unanimous in their condemnation: from Henry James' gentle comment, 'M. Zola reasons less powerfully than he represents' ('The Art of Fiction', *Longman's Magazine*, Sept. 1884, p. 502), to George Moore's witticism branding Zola 'a striking instance of the insanity of commonsense' ('A Visit to Médan', *Confessions of a Young Man*, London, 1926, p. 267), to Edmund Gosse's adjectives: 'grotesque, violent and narrow' ('The Limits of Realism in Fiction', *Forum*, June 1890), to Hemmings' recent description of Zola's doctrine as 'infantile' and 'unbelievably naïve' (*Emile Zola*, Oxford, 1953, p. 109). In the face of this universal censure there is no need to pick further holes in the already threadbare fabric of Naturalist theory. To equate the arts with the sciences and to foist the scientific method on to the creative artist was patently absurd, and this fundamental flaw was to make the doctrine untenable. In the impossibility of its tenets Naturalism contains the seeds of its dissolution. But there were chinks in the logical armour. Zola's favourite phrase, 'Une oeuvre d'art est un coin de la nature vu à travers un tempérament'[1] ('a work of art is a segment of nature seen through the eyes of a certain temperament') admits a far greater degree of subjectivity than his theory strictly permits. To make allowance for the eye of the observer is in effect to depart from the Naturalistic doctrine, and as we shall see, it proved the thin end of a sizeable wedge.

Given the narrowness of Naturalist theory and the mediocrity of many of its adherents in France, it is not surprising that the movement petered out before long. Huysmans was the first to defect to 'spiritual Naturalism' and eventually to a form of mysticism; he was followed by Maupassant, who had always been a disciple of Flaubert rather than of Zola. Another blow was struck in 1887 by the *Manifeste des Cinq*, a manifesto by five obscure writers who voiced the general indignation at Zola's excesses in *La Terre* (*The Soil*). By 1891, when Huret took a kind of literary opinion poll, there was almost unanimous agreement that Naturalism was dead. 'C'était une impasse, un tunnel bouché' ('It was a dead-end, a blocked tunnel') was Huysman's verdict (J. Huret, *Enquête sur l'évolution littéraire*, Paris, 1891, p. 178). Only Zola's faithful friend, Alexis, replied by telegram: 'Naturalisme pas mort. Lettre suit' ('Naturalism not dead. Letter following'). But even Zola had by then, if truth be told, defected in practice.

---

[1] This formula recurs several times in Zola's criticism: in *Mes haines* (1866), in the *Salon de 1866* and in *Le Naturalisme au théâtre*, essay in the volume *Le Roman Expérimental*, Paris 1923, p.111. The earlier version in Zola's art criticism (1866) had the word 'creation' in place of 'nature'.

ENGLAND

The picture of Naturalism in England is a complete contrast to that in France. In England there was never a Naturalist movement as such, i.e. there were no groups or manifestos, only a few scattered works, mainly in the 1890s, by Gissing, George Moore, Morrison, Whiteing. Many so-called Naturalist works were frankly second-rate and have long been forgotten (who knows of, let alone reads, Wedmore's *Renunciations*, Crackanthorpe's *Wreckage*, Harland's *Mlle Miss* or 'Egerton's *Keynotes*?). So much so that the term 'Naturalist' has less relevance to English literature than to most others.

Why is this? After all, there was at least as much, if not more, Realism in nineteenth-century England as in France. Unfortunately, the literary realm is not determined by the laws of cause and effect, nor is it amenable to pure logic. Thus the powerful current of Realism, which in France encouraged the rise of Naturalism, seems perversely to have militated against it in England. As Auerbach has shown in *Mimesis*, Realism had been the very foundation of English art for a long time; it is certainly evident in Shakespeare, Defoe, Fielding, Hogarth, and indeed in several of the English Romantic poets, such as Byron, Wordsworth and Scott. So Realism was ingrained in the English tradition and was an accepted part of serious writing at a period when it was not admissible in France except in the 'lower' genres. This strong indigenous tendency toward Realism meant in turn that the great nineteenth-century Realists – Jane Austen, Dickens, Thackeray, the Brontës, Trollope, Mrs Gaskell, George Eliot – were less startlingly new in England than on the Continent, where they made a great impact. The extent to which Realism was accepted in England is suggested by G. H. Lewes' well-known antithesis between 'Realism' and 'Falsism' which sprang from the assumption that Realism is 'the basis of all Art' ('Realism in Art', *Westminster Review* lxx (Oct. 1858), p. 493). In this climate of opinion realistic works made nothing like the stir they did in France with the prosecution of Flaubert for *Madame Bovary* or the ostracizing of Courbet and the Impressionists. And because of this greater calm in England there was far less aggressive momentum to Realism, and far less urge to take it to its extremes than in France.

The innate English dislike of extremes may also account for the cool reception given to Zola, most of whose major novels were translated between 1884 and 1900. This is not the place to go into this topic which has been covered in W. C. Frierson's article 'English controversy over Realism in fiction 1885–95' (*PMLA* xliii (1928), pp. 533–50). Suffice it to say that Zola's depressing view of man and his 'filthy' method provoked much moral indignation and even resulted in a motion in the House of Commons deploring the importation of demoralizing literature, sponsored by a Mr Smith of the Vigilance Association. Some voices were raised in Zola's favour, but the large circulating libraries, which had such a stranglehold on the fiction market, never abated their hostility, a minor economic fact which may well have deterred aspiring English Naturalists as it did George Moore. Scientific determinism never caught on in England in spite of Spencer and some interest in Comte's Positivism. However, in the last resort, the English writers remained true to their own tradition of a realism spiced with humour and keenly aware of human oddities with only an occasional passing glance at Naturalism.

UNITED STATES OF AMERICA

In the U.S.A. Naturalism is even more closely linked to social and economic changes than in Europe, perhaps because these changes were more rapid and more radical in this new nation. The victory of the North over the South that ended the Civil War in

1865 meant far more than the abolition of slavery. In the long run it amounted to the triumph of industrial capitalism over the traditional agrarian economy. As in Europe, industrialization brought great mechanical and material advances but also extremely severe difficulties in the form of labour disputes, economic depression and strikes that erupted in violence, all of which feature prominently in the literature of the period. Political corruption was rife in many cities where the 'Robber Barons' manipulated business so as to increase the wealth of the rich by excluding the little man and exploiting the labourer. By the last two decades of the century there was widespread disenchantment, as in France after 1870 and in Germany toward the turn of the century. In the U.S.A. it took a special form: disillusionment with the dream of success, prosperity and happiness that had drawn many immigrants to the U.S.A. The collapse of this predominantly agrarian myth brought Americans up against harsh realities with a very sharp shock.

American Naturalism grew in direct response to these native social and economic problems. Often the dire struggles of the poor and/or the machinations of the capitalists are the theme of Naturalist writing as, for instance, in the novels of Dreiser or the short stories of Stephen Crane, or in Steinbeck's *Grapes of Wrath* (1939) which shows how the large powerful combines took over the small holdings, leaving the tenants destitute and homeless. In this way American Naturalism owes more to local factors than to outside influences, and it is worth recalling the so-called 'local colour' tendencies of the 1870s and 1880s which carried on into Naturalism, though with certain shifts of emphasis. To be sure, Darwin, Marx, Comte and Spencer also made an impact, but not with the same immediacy as across the Atlantic. The effect of Zola is not easy to assess either, partly because of the conflicting statements made by some of the American Naturalists (e.g. Dreiser, Crane) and partly because of contradictions in the reception he was given. He was first met with hostility largely on

GROUPS AND THEORIES 35

moral grounds and later, particularly after his defence of Dreyfus, greeted as a great moral figure and social critic. Similarly, his works were frequently translated from 1878 onwards; however, because of the absence of copyright safeguards in the U.S.A. at that time, many of these so-called translations were merely bowdlerized adaptations. By and large it would seem that Zola evoked a fair amount of interest, but except for Frank Norris, he was 'l'agent d'une libération plutôt qu'un modèle' ('the instrument of liberation rather than a pattern') – that is the conclusion of A. J. Salvan in *Zola aux Etats-Unis* (Providence, Rhode Island, 1943, p. 185).

Because American Naturalism arose out of social and economic problems and because there was no single dominant influence, it presents a different aspect from the European Naturalist movement. In contrast to both France and Germany Naturalism in the U.S.A. was much less of a movement as such. There were no clear groups united by common aims and manifestos. In the U.S.A. it is more a matter of successive waves of writers, or perhaps it would be more accurate to speak of generations since there is a great variety of approach within each wave. So the first wave, spanning from about the mid-1880s to the closing years of the century, includes Hamlin Garland (1860–1940), Stephen Crane (1871–1900) and Frank Norris (1870–1902), writers of very different character and calibre. The second generation, after 1900, is an even more curiously assorted bunch: Theodore Dreiser (1871–1945), Jack London (1876–1916), John Steinbeck (1902–68), Sinclair Lewis (1885–1950), Upton Sinclair (1878–1968), Sherwood Anderson (1876–1941) and James T. Farrell (1904–   ). In fact the attempt to discern groupings in American Naturalism is hardly helpful because they never really existed. And when these writers commented on their art it was rather in letters, autobiographies and casual marginalia than in formal manifestos. Such little programmatic writing as there was hardly had much effect on American Naturalism. Garland in *Crumbling Idols* (1894) coupled his condemnation of the old with a demand for originality and Americanism in literature, while Norris' *Responsibilities of the Novelist* (1903), in spite of the weighty title, is merely a series of articles written at his publisher's behest in great haste.

This relative freedom from theory, certainly as compared to Europe, meant that Naturalism in America was a less well-defined or organized movement than in France and Germany. This proved largely to its advantage. Thus American Naturalism, extending from the mid-1880s well into the twentieth century, had a far longer life-span than its European counterparts which strangled themselves with their own theories. The expansiveness was not only temporal either; American Naturalism is altogether characterized by a certain flexibility, notoriously lacking in Europe, and a source of strength across the Atlantic. Determinism, for instance, took only slow and partial root in the U.S.A. so that the worst extremes were avoided. Documentation tended to arise naturally out of the writers' acquaintance with a particular milieu rather than from dogged note-taking. On the other hand, this fluidity creates serious difficulties for the literary historian, especially in distinguishing Naturalism from Realism. Not without reason is the American Naturalism of the early twentieth century often called 'new realism'. There was a continuity of development that amounted to an intermingling. Bowron in his illuminating article on 'Realism in America' uses the vivid image of Realism 'stumbling across the threshold of Naturalism'. Inconclusive though it may seem, there is no alternative but to accept the fact that Naturalism in the U.S.A. was not primarily a literary concept; it was a view of man in society and a style of writing in consonance with the age and this is why it appears in so many diverse writers over such a long period. It was both less and more than Naturalism in Europe.

GERMANY

The most complex and diffuse Naturalist movement was that in Germany. The later 1880s and particularly the 1890s were a time of intense activity in both theory and creative writing. The immense energy of German Naturalism, specially at its beginnings, is perhaps a parallel to the country's upsurge after its unification in 1871. The processes and consequences of industrialization were reinforced by the political and psychological changes following unification; development was extraordinarily rapid in the growth of population, the boom of industry and foreign trade, the establishment of the first German colonies and, in the social sector, the introduction of workers' insurance, compulsory further education and subsidies for opera and drama. As far as Naturalism is concerned, this dynamism burst forth in a plethora of journals such as the *Berliner Monatshefte, Die Kunstwart, Kritische Waffengänge, Die Gesellschaft* and *Freie Bühne für modernes Leben*, societies like *Durch* and the *Verein Freie Bühne*. In addition to the profusion of ideas discussed in these (and other) journals and at meetings of the various groups, a number of important volumes of literary theory were published: Bleibtreu's *Die Revolution der Literatur* (1886), Bölsche's *Die naturwissenschaftlichen Grundlagen der Poesie* (*The Scientific Foundations of Poetry*, 1887), *Die Kunst: ihr Wesen und ihre Gesetze* (*Art: its Nature and its Laws*) by Arno Holz in 1890, to mention only the main ones. As the first major work of Naturalism, Hauptmann's play *Vor Sonnenaufgang*, did not appear till 1889, it is apparent that at the outset German Naturalism was rather top-heavy with theorizing. The umpteen manifestos and proclamations, even when they are as beautifully presented as in E. Ruprecht's indispensable *Literarische Manifeste des deutschen Naturalismus*, are confusing, largely because of the great variety of objectives they put forward. There was in fact little homogeneity in German Naturalism. Of the two main groups, the smaller one, centred on Michael Georg Conrad (1846–1927) in Munich, wrote novels in the wake of Zola, whereas the Berliners, who included Arno Holz (1863–1929), Gerhart Hauptmann (1862–1946) and Hermann Sudermann (1857–1928), concentrated on drama. But the real difficulty is not so much the split between these two groups as the constant elaboration of Naturalist theory in the continued discussions throughout the period. Since it is not possible – nor indeed rewarding – in a monograph of this length to go into minute detail, I propose to outline only the main trends and ideas.

A strong impulse for the unfolding of German Naturalism came from abroad. Ibsen and Tolstoy are frequently cited by the German Naturalists as influential models, and Dostoievsky and Strindberg were hardly less important. On Zola opinion was sharply divided, more so even than in the U.S.A. In some ways the pattern is similar; the initial hostility on account of Zola's Satanic immorality, the slow change as enthusiastic voices were raised, the translations in increasing number from 1880 onwards – all this is fully chronicled in W. H. Root's *German Criticism of Zola 1875–93* (New York, 1931). But in two respects the Germans went beyond the standard reactions in their response to Zola: firstly in their criticism of his theory, not because it went too far, but because it did not go far enough and in the word 'temperament' (in the definition 'Une oeuvre d'art est un coin de la nature vu à travers un tempérament') left the door wide open for subjectivity. This was to be the starting-point of Holz's theories, as we shall see. If, however, Zola was only a nebula ('ein Nebelstern') as a theoretician, he was a glittering star as a creative writer: the German Naturalists were among the earliest to formulate this modern judgement on Zola, although this did not stop them from chewing over his theory *ad nauseam*.

To present German Naturalism as shaped solely by influences from abroad would be misleading. Its relationship to earlier native literature was also important in spite, or because, of its very ambivalence. A strident note of revolt against the insipid 'coffee-party' writing of the immediate past rings out from many of the manifestos. And it is true that nineteenth-century German Realism – Poetic Realism, as it is so appropriately called – was a milk-and-water concoction compared to the more potent brews in France and England. For this reason the German Naturalists found their antecedents further back: in the politically activist *Jungdeutschland* (*Young Germany*) movement that preceded the 1848 revolution, and specially in the dynamic *Sturm und Drang* (*Storm and Stress*) of the 1770s. They saw themselves as revolutionaries, *die Jüngstdeutschen* (*the Youngest Germans*), intent on a renewal of German literature such as the *Storm and Stress* had achieved. There is therefore an element of patriotic fervour in German Naturalism, not apparent anywhere else, and stemming no doubt from the recent national unification. What is more, this patriotic strain often finds expression in high-flown dithyrambs, strangely at variance with Naturalism's scientific sobriety.

The most famous contribution to German Naturalist theory came from Arno Holz in the following law: 'Die Kunst hat die Tendenz, wieder die Natur zu sein. Sie wird sie nach Masstabe ihrer jeweiligen Reproduktionsbedingungen und deren Handhabung.' ('Art has the tendency to be nature again. It becomes nature in proportion to the conditions for imitation and the way they are handled.') (*Die Kunst: ihr Wesen und ihre Gesetze*, reprinted in Ruprecht, *Literarische Manifeste des deutschen Naturalismus*, pp. 210–11.) This dictum is obviously modelled on scientific 'laws', although the German Naturalists on the whole were less insistent on the exact parallel with the sciences than the French. Holz, however, even reduced his law to the equation: 'art $=$ nature $-$ x', x standing for any deficiency in the artist's imitative skill. This equation, so Holz tells us, was formulated from his observations of a child's attempts to draw a soldier; the fact that the drawing was unrecognizable as a soldier is attributed entirely to the failure of the child's mimetic powers. Holz, at least in his theory, allows imagination no role whatsoever; indeed, he objects to Zola's formula on the grounds that the word 'temperament' admits the artist's personal view. Holz's brand of Naturalism consciously sought to eliminate this totally; art was to be as exact a reproduction as could be achieved of man in his milieu. This photo-phonographic ideal Holz called *konsequenter Naturalismus* (literally: 'consequent', i.e. logical, all-out Naturalism). Logical and all-out it certainly was, but hardly practicable as art. In this super-Naturalism speech, for instance, was to be notated with every minute detail of hesitation, repetition, pause to puff a cigarette, cough or clear one's throat – *Sekundenstil* ('second-by-second style') recorded it all faithfully. This is plainly mimetism *ad absurdum*, interesting less as an art form than as an illustration of one of the dangers inherent in Naturalism.

Although few enough writers actually tried to put this theory into practice according to the letter of the law, it did have a wide effect on German Naturalism by its emphasis on form and language. These aspects had been largely neglected by the French and the American Naturalists in their concentration on the content, the picture of man determined by outside forces, portrayed predominantly in the amorphous form of the novel. German Naturalism, in contrast, is strongest in drama, partly under the impact of Ibsen and Strindberg and partly because of the importance attached to language and form. Hence Germany is also the only country where lyric poetry was attempted under the banner of Naturalism. Its main exponent was Holz himself in jagged, rhythmic verse that deliberately broke with the old tradition of smooth and elegant word-music. These poems may be included with Naturalism only in so far as they too seem to partake of the new science-dominated, impersonal approach, preferring 'truth' to 'beauty'. But by their very nature Naturalism and the lyric are not the happiest marriage-partners; it could well be argued that

GROUPS AND THEORIES 41

they are mutually exclusive, and that these German poems should more properly be assigned to the beginnings of Expressionism.

German Naturalism was thus intense, violent and extreme, and perhaps for that very reason, short-lived. As early as 1891 Hermann Bahr was writing of the 'Überwindung des Naturalismus' ('the overcoming of Naturalism') and hailing the advent of a 'Frühling einer neuen Romantik' ('spring of a new Romanticism') after the reign of the purely factual (*Magazin für Literatur*, 1891; reprinted in Ruprecht, *op. cit.*, p. 245.) German Naturalism had, like its French predecessor, only more so, carried the seeds of its dissolution within itself, and not just in the extremism of Holz's theories. For as well as this down-to-earthness gone mad, it contained a considerable streak of idealism, of which its nationalistic fervour is one facet. Its hopes for the future of society and of literature, though clothed in scientific verbiage, are curiously reminiscent of those of the German Romantics. Fundamentally it is much the same high-flown idealism. So it is hardly surprising that most of the leading German Naturalists, including Holz and Hauptmann, rapidly developed away from Naturalism. The movement was, to quote Bahr again 'ein Zwischenakt' ('an interlude'), vital none the less both for the works it produced and for the stimulus it gave to the development of German literature.

4
The Creative Works

THE NOVEL

Naturalism found its chief outlet in the novel (except in Germany, whose contribution to the genre is small but significant, as we shall see). In its concentration on the narrative Naturalism was following on its heritage from the great nineteenth-century novels of Realism. Tolstoy, Dostoievsky, Balzac, Stendhal, Flaubert, Dickens, George Eliot, Mrs Gaskell: these are the writers to whom the Naturalist novelists acknowledged their debt as much as to Darwin and Taine. It is from this combination of Realist tradition and scientific innovations that the Naturalist novel sprang.

The task of definition is made difficult by the large number of novels to which the tag 'Naturalist' has been applied over the past hundred years. They vary greatly in quality from works of lasting literary worth to cheap, sensationalist exploitations of a lucrative formula. In so far as it is possible to generalize at all, given this mass of material, the Naturalist novel is one in which an attempt is made to present with the maximum objectivity of the scientist the new view of man as a creature determined by heredity, milieu and the pressures of the moment. Whatever the inadequacies of this definition, it does point to the interdependence of matter and manner, both of which are drawn from the sciences. All too often the label 'Naturalist' is attached to a work – and this is equally true of drama – merely because its subject is of a type associated with Naturalism, such as slum life or alcoholism or sexual depravity. It is vital to realize that true literary Naturalism is at least as much a question of method as of subject; only when the writer treats his subject with the objectivity of the analytical scientist, can we speak of Naturalism. This criterion, of course, raises considerable difficulties, as we shall see immediately, but we must accept it because it is the one put forward by the Naturalists themselves.

The prototype of the Naturalist novel is Zola's *Thérèse Raquin* (1867). It could hardly lay claim to fame for its plot which must be as old as the art of story-telling; it is, in short, a tale of the adultery between Thérèse and Laurent, their murder of her husband, Camille, which they pass off as an accidental drowning, and the remorse which eventually leads them to the double suicide on which the novel ends. The originality of *Thérèse Raquin* lies in the handling of this unexceptional material. Thérèse and Laurent are presented not as human beings with thoughts, feelings and consciences but as organisms of flesh, blood and nerves. Hence Zola's statement in the preface to the novel that these are animals devoid of soul. Thérèse and Laurent are shown at the mercy of their instincts, which drive them relentlessly first towards each other and then after the murder away from each other. Their behaviour is determined by their physiological, inherited constitution: Laurent is 'sanguine', Thérèse 'nervous'. Their early upbringing, particularly in the case of Thérèse, whose passions have been systematically repressed, helps to explain their actions. An equally important factor is the stifling environment, the dark, musty shop where Thérèse is cooped up with her domineering mother-in-law. Under these circumstances Thérèse's attraction to the strong, coarse Laurent is like a chemical reaction, and thus far the scientific motivation is entirely convincing. Less successful, to my mind, is the attempt to portray Thérèse's and Laurent's remorse as a physical disorder. Laurent's hallucinations and Thérèse's tremblings are all attributed to movements of their blood and nerves, and their effect on each other:

La nature sèche et nerveuse de Thérèse avait agi d'une façon bizarre sur la nature épaisse et sanguine de Laurent. Jadis, aux jours de passion, leur différence de tempérament avait fait de cet homme et de cette femme un couple puissamment lié, en établissant entre eux une sorte d'équilibre, en complétant pour ainsi dire leur organisme. L'amant donnait de son sang, l'amante de ses nerfs, et ils vivaient l'un dans l'autre, ayant besoin de leurs baisers pour régulariser le mécanisme de leur être. Mais un détraquement venait de se produire, les nerfs surexcités de Thérèse avaient dominé. Laurent s'était trouvé tout d'un coup jeté en plein éréthisme nerveux; sous l'influence ardente de la jeune femme, son tempérament était devenu peu à peu celui d'une fille secouée par une névrose aigue. Il serait curieux d'étudier les changements qui se produisent parfois dans certains organismes, à la suite de circonstances déterminées. Ces changements, qui partent de la chair, ne tardent pas à se communiquer au cerveau, à tout l'individu.

(Thérèse's dry, nervous temperament had acted in a strange way on Laurent's coarse, sanguine nature. In the past, in the days of their passion, the difference in their temperament had turned this man and this woman into a strongly linked couple by setting up a sort of balance between their organisms, each completing the other. The lover gave of his blood, the mistress of her nerves, and they lived in each other, needing their kisses to regularize the mechanism of their being. But a breakdown had now occurred; Thérèse's over-excited nerves had become dominant. Laurent had suddenly found himself thrown into a state of nervous erethism; under the young woman's fiery influence his temperament had gradually become that of a young girl undermined by an acute neurosis. It would be interesting to study the changes sometimes produced in certain organisms as the result of specific circumstances. These changes, which start from the body, soon extend to the mind, to the entire individual.)

(Livre de Poche edition, Paris, 1968, pp. 158–9)

This passage – and there are many like it in *Thérèse Raquin* – shows how Zola tried to give a purely physiological interpretation to what we should call the pangs of conscience. His phraseology is medical, his approach that of the scientist observing a chemical

THE CREATIVE WORKS 45

reaction in a test-tube without either moral judgement or emotional sensitivity. This comes as close as is possible to the fulfilment of the Naturalist proposition. But even *Thérèse Raquin* cannot remain within its self-imposed limits: the narrator does not remain totally objective (is not his voice heard at the end of the passage quoted above?); Thérèse and Laurent do suffer remorse and not just physical disorders; and surely they do, subconsciously perhaps, take an active step in murdering Camille and are not mere puppets at the mercy of outer determinant forces. Not surprisingly the prototype of the Naturalist novel already comes up against certain features of Naturalist theory which were to prove untenable and indeed undesirable in a work of art.

With *Les Rougon-Macquart* Zola intended to continue the manner of *Thérèse Raquin*. *Les Rougon-Macquart* is the collective title given to a series of twenty novels written between 1871 and 1893: *La Fortune des Rougon* (1871), *La Curée* (1871), *Le Ventre de Paris* (1873), *La Conquête de Plassans* (1874), *La Faute de l'abbé Mouret* (1875), *Son Excellence Eugène Rougon* (1876), *L'Assommoir* (1877), *Une Page d'amour* (1878), *Nana* (1880), *Pot-Bouille* (1882), *Au Bonheur des dames* (1883), *La Joie de vivre* (1884), *Germinal* (1885), *L'Oeuvre* (1886), *La Terre* (1887), *Le Rêve* (1888), *La Bête humaine* (8190), *L'Argent* (1891), *La Débâcle* (1892), *Le Docteur Pascal* (1893).[1] Each of these novels is complete in itself and at the same time connected to the others. The link is provided by the sub-title of the series: 'Histoire naturelle et sociale d'une famille sous le Second Empire' ('Natural and social history of a family under the Second Empire'). The Rougons and the Macquarts are two branches of a large family whose progress is traced through five generations (Zola even drew a genealogical tree). Their 'natural history' comes in the role of heredity which is much to the fore in *Les Rougon-Macquart* in an amazing sequence

[1] All the novels have been translated into English but English titles are not given because they vary from one translation to another.

of mental and physical diseases. The 'social history' emerges from the many professions and occupations in which the members of the family engage: agriculture, law, mining, medicine, prostitution, banking, the railways, property speculation, laundering, the army, the retail trade, government, the markets, art, etc. Each field is 'documented' with astonishing virtuosity so that we are aware, in the *Rougon-Macquart* series, both of the effect of milieu on the individual and of the social climate of France at that period. These novels truly fulfil the Naturalist demand that the work of art should be a 'human document'. In this as in the essentially physiological view of man and the attempted objectivity *Les Rougon-Macquart* is the outstanding achievement of Naturalism in the novel. This does not mean either that all the novels in the series are equally successful artistically, or that all are consistently Naturalistic. Some, notably *Une Page d'amour*, *La Joie de vivre* and *Le Rêve*, are removed from Naturalism through their lyricism, and even the most characteristic of the series, *L'Assommoir*, *Germinal*, *La Terre* and *Nana*, are esteemed nowadays for their powerfully poetic vision of the commonplace rather than for their precise documentation of heredity and milieu, important though this is. For a change has been taking place in the evaluation of Zola: while his theories are increasingly ridiculed, his novels come to be appreciated more and more – but as the works of a poet rather than of a doctrinal Naturalist. In *Les Rougon-Macquart*, as in *Thérèse Raquin*, Zola put his theories into practice only partially. Far from being a criticism, this is a praise of his writing; Zola's greatness lies in that he transcends the limits of his theory through his poetic imagination. As E. M. Grant has so admirably summarized it (*Emile Zola*, p. 164), '*Les Rougon-Macquart* are the work of a realist and a romantic, or a prose writer and a poet, of an objective historian and a visionary.'

I have dealt at some length with *Thérèse Raquin* and *Les Rougon-Macquart* because they reveal certain common features of the

THE CREATIVE WORKS 47

Naturalist novel as regards form, subject matter and method. Under these three headings we can now consider other novels of the period in an attempt to characterize the novel of Naturalism.

Taking form first, it quickly becomes apparent to the reader that the phrase 'roman expérimental' is highly misleading. These are *not* 'experimental' novels in the sense in which we use the word in English today of Joyce, Virginia Woolf, Kafka, or Faulkner. The Naturalist novel by and large is straightforward, indeed dull, in its narrative technique, rarely departing from nineteenth-century conventions. Its 'experimentation' is directed towards man, who is manipulated as in an experiment in the scientific laboratory. This leads to an emphasis on content and a concomitant neglect of form and style. From Brunetière onwards critics have attacked the Naturalists for their carelessness in construction and language without realizing that these matters seemed quite unimportant to them. They aimed for truth, not artistry; the novel – or drama – must offer a 'slice of life', not a structured artifice. For this reason the Naturalists preferred the amorphous form of the novel, the most flexible of the literary genres, and for this reason also their novels tend to be shapeless and stylistically undistinguished, although there are, as to every such generalization, exceptions. Often the characteristically drawn-out form of the Naturalist novel stems from the desire to trace the evolution of a human being from his origins and through the effects of milieu and circumstances. And since life offers no convenient solutions, we get none from the Naturalist novel, which not infrequently leaves its protagonists in mid-air to continue their endless struggle.

Only in Germany was there any real experimentation with form as we understand it. The German Naturalists were, as we have seen, much more interested in formal problems than any other group; as a result they focused more on drama than on the novel, and the few worthwhile narrative works they produced show a distinct inclination towards the dramatic. This is very evident in

Theodor Fontane's (1819–98) late novels *Effi Briest* (1895) and *Der Stechlin* (1897) with their reliance on subtle dialogue, however sceptical Fontane may have been about doctrinal Naturalism in other respects. The spoken word is so much to the forefront of Johannes Schlaf's and Arno Holz's *Papa Hamlet* (1889), the linking narrative so similar to stage directions that this 'Skizze' ('sketch'), as the authors called it, could almost as well be assigned to the dramatic genre. Holz and Schlaf posited that the Naturalistic narrative should be mainly in dialogue in order to attain the highest degree of objectivity. Speech, including the phonetic notation of personal peculiarities, is used as the means of characterization; the written word in *Papa Hamlet* looks like a transcript of a tape-recording:

> Der kleine Fortinbras jappte!
> Sein Köpfchen hatte sich ihm hinten ins Genick gekrampft, er bohrte es jetzt verzweifelt nach allen Seiten.
> 'Na? Willst du nu, oder nich? – – Bestie!!'
> 'Aber – Niels! Um Gottes willen! Er hat ja wider den – Anfall!'
> 'Ach was! Anfall! – – Da! Friss!!'
> 'Herrgott, Niels...'
> 'Friss!!!'
> 'Niels!' –
> 'Na? Bist du – nu still? – Bist du – nu still? Na?! Na?!'
> 'Ah Gott! Ach Gott, Niels, was, was – machst du denn bloss?! Er, er – schreit ja gar nicht mehr! Er . . . Niels!!'
> Sie war unwillkürlich zurückgeprallt. Seine ganze Gestalt war vornübergeduckt, seine knackenden Finger hatten sich krumm in den Korbrand gekrallt. Er stierte sie an. Sein Gesicht war aschfahl.
> 'Die... L–ampe! Die... L–ampe! Die... L–ampe!'
> 'Niels!!!'
> Sie war rücklings vor ihm gegen die Wand getaumelt.
> 'Still! Still! K–lopft da nicht wer?'
> Ihre beiden Hände hinten hatten sich platt über die Tapete gespreizt, ihre Knie schlotterten.
> 'K–lopft da nicht wer?'

Er hatte sich jetzt noch tiefer geduckt. Sein Schatten über ihm pendelte, seine Augen sahen jetzt plötzlich weiss aus.

Eine Diele knackte, das Öl knisterte, draussen auf die Dachrinne tropfte das Tauwetter.

Tipp —
— — — — — — — — — — — — — — — — — — — —Tipp — — — — — — — — — — — — — —
— — — — — — — — — — Tipp —
— —Tipp — — — — — — — —
— —

(Little Fortinbras was yapping!

His small head was drawn back in a cramp, he jerked it desperately from side to side.

'Well? Do you want to, or not? — — Beast!!'

'But — Niels! For heaven's sake! He is having a — fit again!'

'Nonsense! Fit! — — There! Eat!!'

'Heavens, Niels . . .'

'Eat!!!'

'Niels!' —

'Well? Are you — quiet now? Well? Are you — quiet now? Well?! Well?!'

'Oh my God! oh my God, Niels, what, what — are you doing?! He, he — isn't screaming at all any more! He . . . Niels!!'

She had instinctively startled back. His whole figure was bent forward, his snapping fingers had curled round the edge of the basket. He was staring at her. His face was ashgrey.

'The . . . l–amp! The . . . l–amp! The . . . l–amp!'

'Niels!!!'

She had reeled back before him to the wall.

'Quiet! quiet! Isn't someone kno–cking?'

Both her hands were spreadeagled flat against the wallpaper, her knees were shaking.

'Isn't someone kno–cking?'

He had bent still lower. His shadow above him was swaying, his eyes suddenly looked white.

A floorboard creaked, the oil crackled, outside the thawing ice dripped on to the gutter.

Tipp —
— — — — — — — — — — — — — — — — — —Tipp — — — — — — — — — — — — — — —
— — — — — — — — —-Tipp —
— Tipp — —
— —)

(W. Linden, *Naturalismus*, pp. 161–2)

As an artistic experiment and as a forerunner of twentieth-century linguistic adventures *Papa Hamlet* is one of the most fascinating products of the Naturalist movement. It comes remarkably close, closer probably than *Thérèse Raquin*, to satisfying the theoretical demands of Naturalism. But in its lack of shape and development, its monotony of tone and its incoherence it reveals the serious pitfalls awaiting the truly Naturalist novel.

In subject matter Naturalism in both novel and drama is commonly associated with the portrayal of the working classes, *Armeleutepoesie* ('the poetry of the poor'). The Naturalists certainly wanted to encompass the whole of human life, and they were acutely conscious of the misery in the slums around the factories. Often a socialist element of moral indignation inspired their writing, although this had to be contained behind a façade of objectivity. Whatever their motives, the Naturalists did choose poverty, deprivation and squalor for their subject matter far more than any of their predecessors; many of the outstanding narratives of Naturalism spring to mind in this context: Zola's *L'Assommoir*, *Germinal* and *La Terre*, Stephen Crane's *Maggie, Girl of the Streets* (1893), Moore's *Esther Waters* (1893), Gissing's *The Nether World* (1889), Somerset Maugham's *Liza of Lambeth* (1897), Steinbeck's *Grapes of Wrath* and *Tortilla Flat* (1936), Holz and Schlaf's *Papa Hamlet*, Morrison's *A Child of the Jago* (1896)[1] and Verga's *Vita dei Campi* (1881). In the light of this list, which could easily be supplemented, it is not surprising that Naturalist writing

---

[1] The 'Jago' was a particularly unsavoury area of London's East End.

has been attacked and shunned because of its 'unpleasantness'. That a work of art has a 'disagreeable' theme is, of course, no criterion for a literary judgement; but it is debatable whether the Naturalists, in their desire to face up to reality and with their social conscience, did not over-emphasize the nastiness of life, thereby toppling into the opposite extreme to the Romantic glorification of beauty, but an extreme none the less. On the other hand, the Naturalists did not write exclusively about the working classes, as is sometimes thought. In Zola's *L'Argent, Son Excellence Eugène Rougon, Une Page d'amour* and *La Curée*, Dreiser's *The Financier* (1912) and *An American Tragedy* (1925), Norris' *Vandover and the Brute* (1905, published 1914) and Thomas Mann's *Buddenbrooks* (1901) the prosperous middle classes are subjected to that characteristic Naturalist scrutiny which takes the lid off the high as well as the lowly.

This in fact is the important point about Naturalist subject matter: that at all levels of society the same guiding principles prevail and all men are shown to be fundamentally alike. The scientific, physiological, mechanistic view of human life is heedless of class; it reduces all men to the same formula – creatures ruled by heredity, milieu and the pressures of the moment. The Naturalists are, to my mind, much more open to attack for their view of man than for the 'unpleasantness' of their themes, which in a sense devolve from their concept of man. Their whole philosophy led them to portray the ordinary man rather than the extraordinary individual who fascinated the Romantics. The individual tends to be an outsider, whereas the Naturalists focus on man *in* his milieu. For this reason the description of milieu features large in Naturalist works, and for this reason too there is often no real 'hero'. The heroic is alien to the scientific view of man: freedom of choice and responsibility for his actions are implicitly denied to a creature determined by forces beyond his control. It is this pessimistic picture of man rather than any innate unpleasantness of theme that makes the Naturalist novel rather depressing reading. And there is, I think, a contradiction between this negative concept of man on the one hand and on the other the belief in social progress that made the Naturalists expose the evils of 'baby-farming', the working conditions of miners, servants, etc. It is, moreover, open to question whether the novel as a form could in the long run continue to centre on a passive, 'determined', unheroic figure such as Clyde Griffiths in *An American Tragedy*. The flatness would be as monotonous as the *Sekundenstil* of *Papa Hamlet*. The Naturalist view of man proves as awkward in artistic practice as its formal programme.

Difficulties arise also in the application of the scientific method to literature. The comparison of the writer to the anatomist or surgeon implied an ideal of total objectivity. The Naturalists went a fair way towards this goal. They chose subjects from the contemporary scene which they could observe (there is no such thing as a Naturalist historical novel); they collected 'documentation' with care and depicted milieu in scrupulous detail, at times overloading their novels with technical matter – one can acquire a reasonable, though now out of date knowledge of mining, laundering, farming, the stock-exchange, printing, the manufacture of pottery, wet-nursing, pick-pocketing, cotton-picking and other useful accomplishments from a diligent reading of Naturalist novels. The dominant tone is that of factual reportage, where things are more important than thoughts, and characters and happenings are seen from the outside, so to speak. But however hard they tried, the Naturalists could not in practice maintain this degree of scientific objectivity. To put it bluntly, the narrator could not be eliminated from the novel. Rarely does he comment openly on his story in the manner of, say, Thackeray; but there are moments when his voice is heard, and he is, of course, present in his very choice of words. It is indeed often the adjectives which break the surface objectivity to express some sympathy or judgement.

This failure to achieve complete objectivity was most fortunate, for how could dispassionate reports be literature? Naturalist theory on this point stemmed from a fallacy; in practice the individual imagination that makes a man an artist was bound to assert itself, as it did.

From this account the Naturalist novel hardly seems attractive. Much criticism has been directed against it, none more cogent than that of Edmund Gosse, who, in his important essay 'The Limits of Realism in Fiction', sees many Naturalists steering an uneasy course between 'the Scylla of brutality' and 'the Charybdis of insipidity'. (Reprinted in G. Becker, *Documents of Modern Literary Realism*, pp. 383–93.) It is easy enough to attack the Naturalist novel on the grounds that its limited view of man led to distortion and repetitiveness, that it is shoddy in form, that it is alternately and at times even simultaneously pedestrian and melodramatic. All these criticisms are justified, certainly as far as the poorer novels of this kind are concerned – the early works of Huysmans and Norris, not to mention the novels of Kretzer, Alberti, Céard, Alexis, Ridge, and Wedmore which are, mercifully, not even in specialist libraries. But lest these reservations deter the potential reader, let it be said outright that many Naturalist novels make absorbing and enjoyable reading; they offer an unusual insight into various milieux, and their straightforward story-telling makes fewer intellectual demands on the reader than a more complex technique might. Many works do avoid the dangers to which the Naturalist novel is prone, and if there are few of great excellence, there are a good number above average competence. Their success often seems related to their departure from the strict canons of Naturalist theory. This tendency is apparent from *Thérèse Raquin* and *Les Rougon-Macquart* onwards, as we have seen. Certain aspects of Naturalist theory, notably the ideal of total objectivity and the 'determined' view of man, quickly proved untenable in practice. The eye of the observer was that of an artist, and his experimental material was the human being in all his irrationality. The work of art had been defined by Zola as 'un coin de la nature vu à travers un tempérament'; in practice that 'temperament' played a far more decisive part than any of the theoreticians of Naturalism had anticipated. So there is a discrepancy between theory and practice in the Naturalist novel which does *not* exclude the imaginative in language and symbolism, or the nobler sides of human nature, or even distinct elements of romance. Almost any of the novels of Zola, or Steinbeck's *Grapes of Wrath*, or Stephen Crane's *Maggie, Girl of the Streets*, or George Moore's *Esther Waters*, or Bennett's *Clayhanger* has some characteristics that reach beyond the confines of Naturalism. The good novel of Naturalism is not a transference of science into art, but rather a marriage of the two, tense at times, often rewarding.

DRAMA

At first sight drama seems a particularly suitable medium for achieving the aims of Naturalism because the stage by its very nature encourages the objective presentation of a slice of life in all its immediacy. But if Realism was to be fulfilled or even transcended by Naturalism, how best could this be done in dramatic terms? If the human being, his actions and reactions, are only comprehensible in the light of his environment and heredity, his mental and physical state at any given moment, and the social pressures being exerted on him, the Naturalist dramatist must devise ways and means of illustrating these conditioning factors. Zola himself could see no reason why the Naturalist formula could not adjust itself to the requirements of drama: 'Le roman analyse longuement, avec une minutie de détails où rien n'est oublié; le théâtre analysera aussi brièvement qu'il le voudra, par les actions et les paroles' ('The novel analyses at length with a minuteness of detail in which nothing is forgotten; the theatre will analyse as briefly as it wishes by means of actions and words'). (Zola, *Le*

THE CREATIVE WORKS 55

Naturalisme au théâtre, p. 149, translated in Becker, *Documents of Modern Literary Realism*, pp. 224–5.) But deprived of the novelist's scope for description and analysis, the Naturalist dramatists discovered that what was apparently the most appropriate form for realizing the ideal of total clinical objectivity presented them in fact with very considerable problems. In a play there is no room for commentary and explanation; yet it must provide the audience with all the relevant data, with the case histories of characters who must be left to speak for themselves without using the improbable conventions of monologue and aside. In this sense the Naturalist period was one of experimentation in the drama, for here the inherited techniques of Realism were inadequate, whereas in the novel the generally accepted nineteenth-century techniques of narrative could, as we have seen, be adapted with little strain to new ideas and content. Very many aspiring playwrights tried their hand, but only a few, perhaps only Hauptmann, actually succeeded in reconciling the wide preoccupations of Naturalism with the temporally and spatially confined action which a Naturalist play requires.

Even before Zola published his novel *Thérèse Raquin*, two significant plays appeared in Russia. These were *A Bitter Fate* (1859) by Pisemsky (1821–81) (translated in *Masterpieces of the Russian Drama*, edited by George Rapall Noyes (Vol. 1), New York, 1960) and *The Storm* (1860) by his more illustrious contemporary Ostrovsky (1823–86). Both could simply be termed Realist, were it not for the fact that they came as the confirmation of what had become the general trend in Russian drama from 1850 onwards, and distinguished it from the *well-made plays* with which popular French authors such as Scribe, Dumas fils and Sardou inundated the theatres of Europe from about 1830 to 1914. In contrast to these, the Russians favoured the realistic depiction of society on all levels, concentrating on the most individual and therefore least universal aspects of a social milieu. At its best, as in Ostrovsky, this focus on specific ways of life in their local and temporal aspects (what D. S. Mirsky calls 'ethnographical realism') anticipates a characteristic feature of much Naturalist drama. Thus in *The Storm* the futility of struggling against conventional pressures is stressed in the narrow environment of a provincial town where religious superstition, ignorance and family pride drive Katerina Kabanova to suicide when her bigoted and domineering mother-in-law, the embodiment of self-righteous convention, refuses to let her forget a momentary unfaithfulness to her dull, submissive husband. These are of course both pre-Naturalist plays, but one cannot fail to observe in them an insistence on the various factors conditioning the mentality and behaviour of individual human beings, and the allusions to the changes threatening an established way of life as a result of technological progress. Moreover the authenticity of their depiction of provincial life and their sensitive handling of colloquial language are far removed from the sentimentality and artificiality of the Western European Realist theatre of the period.

But Russia's real impact on Naturalist drama did not come until 1886, with Tolstoy's *The Power of Darkness*, which, banned in Russia, was produced in Paris with Zola's backing and with overwhelming success. The artistic integrity of Tolstoy's stark depiction of peasant lust, adultery, infanticide and final public confession ensured this play a central position as the most widely read and performed example of one of the two main trends in Naturalist drama: the unequivocal and authentic depiction of the *state of affairs* prevailing in a section of society of which the average reader or playgoer is or would like to be unaware. Gorky's exposure of deprivation and squalor in the lower reaches of society in *The Lower Depths* (1902) was another Russian example.

The exposure of hidden abuses or the sparking off of a 'ripe situation', both often prompted by an outsider (the 'messenger from the outside world') was also a characteristic feature of the other main trend in Naturalist drama, a development of the *problem drama* of which Ibsen (1828–1906) had been the leading exponent from *Pillars of Society* (1877) to *Rosmersholm* (1886). It is not surprising that problem drama is essentially middle class. In Naturalist peasant or working-class drama the main objective is to bring facts, states of affairs, to the urgent notice of the rest of society (i.e. the playgoer) which is of course mainly middle class. But in problem drama the emphasis is on legal or illegal situations (such as marriage and adultery) which pose grave problems to all concerned – governments, legislators, and society as a whole. Here the dramatist had to take the susceptibilities and prejudices of his audience into account because they were doubtless privately aware of identical problems. Righteous indignation and reforming zeal could certainly be the motives underlying both types of drama, but in the case of the latter, the reactions aroused were bound to be considerably more complex and often more violent.

There is one play which probably produced more violent and complex reactions wherever it was performed than any other and which, rightly or wrongly, is generally remembered today as the most important Naturalist drama. Ibsen's *Ghosts* was published in 1881 and, wherever it went, it was surrounded by controversy. In Germany it was hailed as a breakthrough in modern drama, prompting the finest critic of the Naturalist period, Otto Brahm, to a confession of his aesthetic beliefs: 'Offen und frei liegt alles, nur zuzugreifen hat der Dichter' ('All is now permissible, all the writer need do is set to work') and to a pinpointing of what was so new about it: 'Die unbarmherzige, grelle Wahrheit in der Schilderung menschlicher Charaktere' ('the remorseless and vivid truth of its depiction of human characters'), while in England Shaw, in many ways Brahm's counterpart as the most stimulating intellect committed to the Naturalist cause, let himself go with his provocative and wide-ranging essays in *The Quintessence of Ibsenism*

(1891). Not surprisingly, Ibsen's dramatic raising of the ghosts lurking in middle-class society, his ruthless exposure of the truth beneath the 'social lie', his startling analysis of the workings of heredity in its most unpleasantly clinical form – congenital syphilis – all this led to *Ghosts* playing a part in Naturalist drama equivalent to that played by Zola's *Thérèse Raquin* in the Naturalist novel.

In this capacity the stage career of *Ghosts* was closely associated with the fortunes of the three 'independent theatres' which, along with the later *Moscow Art Theatre* (founded by Danchenko and the great producer Stanislavsky in 1898), played such a vital part in promoting the Naturalist cause by translating its ideals into practical terms: into new techniques of production and acting, and the exploitation of the potentialities of artificial lighting. The first of these independent theatres in date and contemporary renown was the Paris *Théâtre libre* founded in 1887 by André Antoine (1858–1943). Admittedly this venture failed financially, but not before it had produced *Ghosts* (in 1890) and delivered Europe from the dominance of the *well-made play* in the nineteenth-century Realist tradition. Inspired partly by the *Théâtre libre*, a group of enterprising and forward-looking Germans then set up a private association in Berlin to produce contemporary plays without interference from censorship, calling it *Freie Bühne* ('Free Stage'). It opened in September 1889 with a defiant declaration of its practical and aesthetic objectives: a production of *Ghosts*. The same play launched the third of these important Naturalist theatrical ventures, the *Independent Theatre of London*, founded in 1891 by Jack Grein 'to give special performances of plays which have literary and artistic rather than commercial value'.

The reaction to *Ghosts* was most violent in London, probably because England, like America, had much less of a recent Realist theatrical tradition than Russia, France or Germany. Ibsen wanted his play to be produced 'without evading in any way the necessity for complete and ruthless realism' (letter of August 1883). The *Daily Telegraph* described the result as 'an open drain; a loathsome sore unbandaged; a dirty act done publicly'! Only in the light of such hysterical reactions as these can the full excitement of Naturalist drama among contemporary audiences be appreciated. In this way too, *Ghosts* set a precedent; scandal and uproar became justifiably associated with public performances of all-out Naturalist drama, other famous instances being Hauptmann's *Vor Sonnenaufgang* in Berlin (1889), Shaw's *Mrs Warren's Profession* in New York (1905) and Brieux's *Les Avariés* in Paris and Belgium (1901–2).

Ibsen may strike us as having taken over and perfected the unnaturally logical technique of the well-made play, but we would do well to remember that to most contemporaries his plays seemed to illustrate Naturalism in all its aspects. They could scarcely believe their eyes, for what they were seeing on the stage seemed to them a thoroughly authentic representation of real life. Significantly this is still the impression which can be made by good productions of working-class drama – the other main strand of Naturalism. But manners, behaviour and values in middle-class society have changed, and a feeling for period authenticity has had to take the place of contemporary reality in our appreciation and production of the majority of Naturalist plays; indeed this brings home the fact that there has never been a literary movement so exclusively aimed at its own day – perhaps the most viable definition of Naturalism, especially when one turns to its dramatic works. Thus the logical development and ordered pace of the dialogue in *Ghosts* were, in contemporary opinion, an accurate reproduction of late nineteenth-century middle-class conversation. Domestic trivialities did not intrude; life below stairs was equally valid, but it was being treated elsewhere, in Strindberg's *Miss Julie* (1888) or Hauptmann's *Fuhrmann Henschel* (1898) for instance. The milieu itself is immaterial; what made *Ghosts* a central event in

Naturalist drama was twofold. Firstly it dealt with contemporary man in his cultural and social environment. In Mrs Alving's words to Pastor Manders in their long dialogue in Act II:

> It's not just what we inherit from our mothers and fathers that haunts us. It's all kinds of old defunct theories, all sorts of old defunct beliefs, and things like that. It's not that they actually *live* on in us; they are simply lodged there and we cannot get rid of them.
> (Translated by J. W. McFarlane, *The Oxford Ibsen*, Vol. V, p. 384)

Secondly Ibsen was so obviously aware of the central problem of complete objectivity:

> My intention was to try and give the reader an impression of experiencing a piece of reality. But nothing would more effectively run counter to this intention than inserting the author's opinions into the dialogue ... In none of my plays is the author so extrinsic, so completely absent.
> (Letter of 6 January 1882, *ibid.*, p. 476)

In the light of the quotation above, one may well wonder whether he solved the problem any better than Zola. But that was the Naturalist fallacy; the pursuit of the 'illusion of reality'.

The problem play came most into its own in France where, despite the aesthetic preoccupations of the Naturalist novel, it dominated the avant-garde stage throughout the period. Thus formal tradition maintained its hold on even the most adventurous playwrights, receiving a revitalizing injection from Ibsen's own example. But in spite of the number of dramatists stimulated by the *Théâtre libre*, did any really manage to incorporate the Naturalist view of man in satisfying stage works? For instance François de Curel (1854–1928), though hailed as the 'French Ibsen', possessed now largely forgotten qualities which are essentially at variance with the realistic objectivity he ostensibly represented. Thus his admirable play *L'Envers d'une sainte* (1892) reveals how a saintly woman appears in the eyes of her own family; the disparity between appearance and reality is exposed, but much more is at stake than the materialist theories of environment and heredity, and the author's irony takes precedence over carefully documented reality.

The major force in French Naturalist drama is unquestionably Eugène Brieux (1858–1932). Unlike his counterparts in other countries he poses a perplexing problem of assessment. After Ibsen's death, he was ranked by Shaw as the 'most important dramatist west of Russia', and was generally regarded as the equal of Ibsen, Strindberg, Gorky, Chekhov and Hauptmann, the counterpart therefore in French Naturalist drama of Zola. But quite unlike these, he has subsequently lost his reputation entirely. No major dramatist committed himself so singlemindedly to the Naturalist cause, and when in 1897 he produced his finest play *Les trois filles de M. Dupont* (*The Three Daughters of Monsieur Dupont*), it could certainly be said to bring home both the qualities and limitations of French Naturalism in the theatre. The central action is the marriage of 24-year-old Julie Dupont to a banker's son, Antonin Mairaut, to achieve which each set of parents is proud of having duped the other. Money links this plot to the neatly contrasting careers of Julie's older sisters: Caroline, the spinster, who has learnt the 'grief of loneliness' and turned to religion, and Angèle, who was disowned on leaving home and has since experienced 'an excess of disgust, degradation and misery'. Within this framework Brieux's central themes emerge in two scenes between husband and wife. The first, characteristically, is the intolerable nature of prevailing social conditions: (Julie) 'Non, je ne me plains pas des lois, je me plains des moeurs. Notre malheur, vois-tu, ce n'est pas qu'il y ait tel ou tel article du code; notre malheur, c'est qu'on nous ait mariés comme on nous a mariés' ('No, I am not complaining about the laws, I am complaining about social customs. You see, our trouble isn't that the legal system prescribes this or that; our trouble is that they married us in the way they did'). Then, in Act II, Antonin is provoked by his wife into speaking the truth, into unveiling the hypocrisy and turpitude of middle-class marriage, saying in apology for himself 'Je ne suis pas un héros; je suis de mon temps, et ce n'est pas moi qui l'ai fait comme il est' ('I'm not a hero; I belong to my own times and I didn't make them what they are'). But as in all comedies and, Brieux implies, as in the *social comedy* of average life, the abyss is once again patched over, leaving Julie to reflect 'J'avais rêvé mieux; mais il paraît que c'est impossible' ('I dreamt of something better, but it seems it was impossible'). No door slams as in Ibsen's *Doll's House* (1879); life goes monotonously on.

It may not be a great play. But the fact that it lacks many of the qualities we are taught to associate with great drama is precisely what makes it an outstanding example of French Naturalism. Brieux's technique may stem from the Realist tradition, but it is less slick, much less contrived; his presentation of his material is prosaic, devoid of any hint of poetic let alone symbolic dimensions; in this drama of the falsity of illusions and the harshness of truth there is no wild duck, no seagull, no revolver shot and no purple passage. The milieu is everything, and even Julie and Antonin are just average 'little' people; neither rises to 'tragic' heights, the tragedy resides in the social situation of which they are typical products. Yet Brieux's approach is not pessimistic; his mature view of drama is that it can be the means of bringing about a better world by exposing the defects of contemporary society. The problem play or *pièce à thèse* becomes the *useful play*.

By choosing a specific subject for each of his plays, Brieux was able to provide a dramatic survey of contemporary society while remaining aware that, in comparison with the novel, a play is limited in scope. Many typical Naturalist subjects – marriage, divorce, children, the legal system, industrial relations – were dealt with. Then came his two most notorious plays: *Les Avariés* (known in England and America as *Damaged Goods*) in 1901 and *Maternité* in 1903. These are extreme examples of one current in Naturalist drama: the ruthlessly objective and indeed uninhibited exposure of social abuses with a moral and didactic aim to redeem it from the slur of pornography, forcibly reminding one of the similarity of his brand of Naturalist drama to the probing social documentaries of contemporary television. *Maternité* is a set of variations (or case histories) on the problem of population policy (always an issue of concern in France) and, in counterpoint to it, on the question of birth control, and if conventional dramatic form breaks down here, the experimental documentary aspects are even more apparent in *Les Avariés*, a 'physiological study' of the ravages of venereal disease. Act I is simply a consultation between a doctor and a syphilitic; names are not provided. Thus Zola's clinical analogies here found their dramatic fulfilment, though the depersonalized ritual we witness is in many ways closer to Expressionism than to Naturalism as it is generally understood.

But Brieux is virtually forgotten, one of the many casualties of Naturalist literature, and the only French dramatist still remembered as a representative of it is his precursor, Henry Becque (1837–99) with one play *Les Corbeaux* (*The Crows*) of 1882. By French standards this gloomy depiction of the despoliation of a businessman's family after his death by his lawyers, creditors and colleagues is a 'slice of life' so remorselessly harsh that it led to its author being termed a writer of *comédies rosses* (harsh, true-to-life plays).

It is significant that *Les Corbeaux* failed when it was given by the *Freie Bühne* in 1891. In the first place the German Naturalists had already succeeded in perfecting a phonetically realistic rendering of dialogue which left French attempts far behind and which was prompted by Germany's relative lack of linguistic unity and the unavoidable need to include dialect in any Naturalist reproduction of articulate reality. Secondly we are reminded that a translation is no guide to the value of a Naturalist play as such. Precisely because of the German achievement in the field of dramatic language, characteristic speech-patterns, dialectal colouring, verbal gestures, silences, etc., the problems of translation apply to German Naturalism more than to any other and largely account for its otherwise unwarranted neglect outside Germany. Yet this is undoubtedly Germany's greatest contribution to Naturalist writing and was at once audibly apparent in the first great German Naturalist play (produced immediately after *Ghosts* during the *Freie Bühne's* first season): *Vor Sonnenaufgang* (1889) by Gerhart Hauptmann. The mood, especially in Berlin, was ripe. In 1886 a farsighted critic, Julius Hillebrand, had prophesied; 'Aber auch Ibsen in seiner nordischen Kraft und Herbheit ist erst der Marlow, bestimmt, dem künftigen Shakespeare die Wege zu bereiten' ('But even Ibsen, with his nordic strength and harshness, is only a Marlowe, destined to prepare the way for the Shakespeare of the future'). The Germans were alone in seeing that Ibsen would have to be left behind if Naturalism was to realize its full dramatic potential. Such auguries gave Hauptmann an enviable introduction to the German stage; overnight it became obvious that the new Shakespeare had arrived, and nothing has happened since to prove that this conviction was wrong.

German drama had been languishing for some time, but it had already witnessed some remarkable experiments which pointed in the direction which German Naturalism was to take. The *Sturm und Drang* movement of the 1770s has been mentioned; some of its plays do in fact contain many of the external hallmarks of Naturalism (like Lenz's *Die Soldaten* and Wagner's *Die Kindermörderin*, both of 1776). Formal experimentation continued with Grabbe (1801–36) who made a cross-section of the Parisian public the 'hero' of his *Napoleon* (1831), while Büchner (1813–36) presented the sufferings of an inarticulate soldier in a fragmentary sequence of scenes (*Woyzeck*) which, when published in 1879, soon began to stimulate the new techniques which it had anticipated. Even more relevant to the rise of Naturalism in Germany was a play by the Austrian Ludwig Anzengruber (1839–89) called *Das vierte Gebot* ('The Fourth Commandment', by German reckoning!), which in 1877 depicted the pernicious effects of parental example on impressionable teenagers in the urban environment of a large city (Vienna). The violent hostility it encountered from the censorship, the Church, and conservative critics was however overshadowed by the storm which broke over Hauptmann's *Vor Sonnenaufgang* (*Before Sunrise*), in which a progressive teetotal sociologist, Alfred Loth, arrives in a region of rural Silesia recently grown rich through the discovery of coal deposits, to carry out a scientific inquiry into mining conditions, with disastrous results for the girl he falls in love with and abandons on discovering that her family are alcoholics. Helene commits suicide in a last act throughout which her alcoholic sister is giving birth, off-stage, to a stillborn child; a well-known doctor, for whom this was too much – in art as opposed to real life – is reported to have flung some forceps on to the stage and to have walked out of the theatre shouting 'these may come in useful!', a compliment to the degree of Naturalism achieved in Berlin. Indeed the crassness and horror of Hauptmann's realism and the profound humanity of his portrayal of suffering, coupled with his uncanny skill for reproducing the feel of a situation, the intonation of a voice, the latent instincts of a human being, at last revealed what splendours Naturalism was capable of.

Any objective evaluation of Naturalist drama is bound to reach the conclusion that only in Germany did it realize its complete potential, and that only there did it produce plays of conclusive literary merit. Hauptmann followed his brilliant first play with two studies of the still topical themes of incomprehension, loneliness and the inability to communicate, the one situated in a family

(*Das Friedensfest, Reconciliation*, 1890), in many ways anticipating the post-Naturalist work of Pinter, the other concerned with the marriage between an intellectual scientist and a girl of simple integrity broken up by an emancipated woman student (*Einsame Menschen, Lonely People*, 1891). In a sense these were modifications of the middle-class problem play, but then in 1892 came the culmination of Naturalism's proletarian strand with *Die Weber* (*The Weavers*), the classic drama of hunger, strike, and abortive rebellion. In *Die Weber* Hauptmann succeeded where all other Naturalists failed. The greatest Naturalist drama is one in which plot and hero are dispensed with altogether, and in which speech seems to emerge spontaneously from the characters themselves (especially in the original Silesian dialect version *De Waber*). The product of careful documentation and research, it naturally provoked the hostility of the establishment, which in turn ensured its lasting success as the precursor of *Socialist Realism*, in particular through the Russian translation supervised by Lenin himself. *Die Weber* was in fact the unique realization of Naturalism's ideal of bringing social movement to life in all its density and immediacy, with all its complex motivations and implications. Chekhov alone achieved anything analogous, though his themes and approach disqualify him from treatment here.

An important feature of the texts of all these plays is the meticulous description of stage sets (*Milieuschilderung*: depiction of a milieu), a largely extra-theatrical device designed with the reader in mind and clearly related to narrative techniques, the solution therefore to one of the fundamental problems of Naturalist drama (e.g. the page-long stage directions for the superbly handled pub scene in *Die Weber* or even the Silesian countryside in Act I of *Rose Bernd*, which like so much all-out Naturalism anticipates the modern cinema). But Hauptmann was essentially a dramatist and went on to reveal new aspects of his mastery and ability to solve the technical problems which defeated so many of his contem-

THE CREATIVE WORKS 67

poraries. Thus in *Fuhrmann Henschel* (*Drayman Henschel*, 1898) and *Rose Bernd* (1903) he explored the function of sex as a determining factor in human motivation, at the same time daringly relegating so-called dramatic action to the intervals between the acts in accordance with his maxim 'Immer mehr *Undramatisches* dramatisch zu begreifen, ist der Fortschritt' ('Progress means capturing more and more of what is "undramatic" in dramatic terms'). His last great drama in the all-out Naturalist manner was *Die Ratten* (*The Rats*, 1911), now probably his most popular play, which gives us a cross-section of the tragic and comic happenings in a Berlin tenement house and implies an analogy to pre-1914 German society as a whole – *Les Rougon-Macquart* compressed as it were into one play as a final vindication of Naturalist drama. Something less theatrically effective but just as ambitious artistically had meanwhile been achieved by the Naturalist theorist Arno Holz, in collaboration with Johannes Schlaf. *Papa Hamlet* had verged on drama; they now turned their attention to it entirely, making use of their second-by-second technique (*Sekundenstil*) in *Die Familie Selicke* (1890), a bleak evocation of life in an East Berlin tenement house. Schlaf then proceeded alone in *Meister Ölze* (1892) to explore the after-effects of murder in low-class surroundings in what German critics generally regard as the finest dramatic specimen of *konsequenter Naturalismus*. At the opposite extreme there were also the internationally successful and undeniably effective plays of Hermann Sudermann, particularly *Heimat* (*Home*, better known as *Magda*, 1893), in which Naturalism helps conventional realism (and great actresses!) to evoke a successful soprano's return to the upper-middle-class home that almost stifled her youth.

Magda enjoyed great success in England and understandably so, for by English standards it seemed uncompromisingly true to life. Admittedly Shaw (1856–1950) fought hard to change the prevailing taste, hoping to 'persuade even London to take its conscience

F

68 NATURALISM

and its brains with it when it goes to the theatre, instead of leaving them at home with its prayer book', exposing the bogus respectability of slum property owners in *Widowers' Houses* (1892) and provoking moral outrage with *Mrs Warren's Profession* (1894, though not performed until the Lord Chamberlain's prohibition was lifted in 1902), in which he took a 'social subject of tremendous force', declaring that 'drama is no mere setting up of the camera to nature: it is the presentation in parable of the conflict between Man's will and his environment: in a word of problem' (Apology for *Mrs Warren's Profession*, 1902). But as this statement indicates, Shaw soon abandoned even the semblance of Naturalist drama, as did his infinitely more exciting contemporary Strindberg (1849–1912), who had revealed his insight into the paradoxes of Naturalism as early as the *Preface* to his Naturalist play *Miss Julie* (1888). (Reprinted in Becker, *Documents of Modern Literary Realism*, pp. 394–406.) Apart from Galsworthy (*Strife*, 1909), the English-speaking countries produced little that can honestly be termed Naturalism, though the nationally-flavoured realism of the Irish dramatists owes much to it (Synge's *The Playboy of the Western World*, 1907, and Sean O'Casey's early plays). But unexpectedly England has the last word. All-out Naturalism, with its 'emphasis on ways of speaking minutely observed and reproduced, as the social reality of a particular dimension of life' (Raymond Williams, Introduction to D. H. Lawrence, *Three Plays*, Harmondsworth, 1969, p. 11.), produced one last flowering which can still be said to belong to the movement and not to that neo-Naturalism which has marked so much mid-twentieth-century cinema and theatre and which belatedly made London in 1956 capture something of the excitement of Berlin in 1889. This was the set of plays which D. H. Lawrence wrote between 1909 and 1913 in an effort to record the atmosphere in which he grew up, and which have at last come into their own in recent years as the only really satisfying Naturalist drama in English. Gone is any conscious attempt to vindicate the aesthetic theories of Naturalism, yet to read these plays (especially *A Collier's Friday Night*, c. 1909 and *The Daughter-in-Law*, 1912) in conjunction with a translation of Hauptmann is probably the best way of coming to understand what true Naturalist drama is.

5
Conclusion

THE achievements and failures of a literary movement cannot be weighed up, like those of a business enterprise, in a tidy balance-sheet. Nor can the accounts ever be closed, for literary criticism is a process of constant reassessment. This is amply illustrated by the vicissitudes of the Naturalist movement, which was first attacked for its amorality, then valued for its social documentation and more recently is coming to be appreciated for its literary qualities. This so-called 'conclusion' is therefore inevitably an interim and to some extent a personal one: its aim is not to stow away Naturalism once and for all into cold storage but to stimulate thought and discussion.

Naturalism is an extremist movement. It represents an attempt to extend mimetic realism to its furthermost logical limits and it thereby casts the artist into the role of a photo-phonographic recorder of reality. The absurdity of this stance is too apparent to require comment: art is *not* 'nature—x', as Holz would have it, nor does the artist work like the scientist, as Zola maintained. The theories of Naturalism, if taken literally, amount in fact to a formidable anti-aesthetics in their deliberate exclusion of the creative power of the artist's individual imagination. The view of man was too limited and the conception of the artistic process too profoundly erroneous to be conducive to lasting works of art.

Fortunately, with rare exceptions, the adherents of Naturalism did not quite practise what they preached, largely, one suspects, because it proved totally impracticable. The word 'temperament' in Zola's famous definition ('Une oeuvre d'art est un coin de la nature vu à travers un tempérament') was a breach in the line of scientific objectivity. Because the eye of the observer was not an inanimate photographic lens, the picture of reality in each naturalistic work is recognizably individual. The portrait of reality which the Naturalists purported to give soon proves on examination to be a vision of reality. In the very choice of words, i.e. in the translation from reality into art, the artist's individual genius comes into play. And so the practitioners of Naturalism departed from their own theory. To maintain that their writing is personal does not imply autobiographical confessions such as the Romantics produced; it means that each novel or drama clearly bears the stamp of its author in its style as well as in its preoccupations. Images, symbols, and evocative, poetic adjectives insinuated themselves into what set out to be coldly factual accounts; similarly, man's ideals and illusions were re-admitted alongside his heredity, milieu and pressures of the moment. It is not surprising that the greatest writers associated with Naturalism all moved away from it sooner or later. Ibsen's *When We Dead Awaken* (1899), Strindberg's *Dream Play* (1901), Zola's *Une Page d'amour* spring to mind immediately, but even more interesting are those works such as Hauptmann's *Hanneles Himmelfahrt* (1894), Crane's *Maggie, Girl of the Streets*, Steinbeck's *Grapes of Wrath* and Zola's *Germinal* where Naturalism is shot through with poetry. In each case the 'temperament' of a genius has illumined the scientific reality of heredity, milieu and moment, and elevated it into a memorable and moving work of art.

So the paradoxical conclusion emerges that Naturalism succeeded best where it seemed to fail, i.e. where it departed from, or rather outstripped its own intentions. As a serious attempt to bring the arts into line with the sciences it failed, as it was bound to do in so misguided an undertaking. It failed also to put much of its theory into practice because of the innate defects and limitations of that theory. On the credit side, it undoubtedly opened up large new areas of subject matter in the struggles of the working classes and it introduced new modes, particularly of dialogue, which were to be of real importance for twentieth-century literature. Even in the lyric the Naturalists were indirectly pioneers for some of the earliest examples of the poetry of urban life are found in their novels. It could also be claimed that in their exposure of hypocritical moral attitudes and social abuses the Naturalists prefigured twentieth-century literature of commitment. In contrast and in opposition to the Aestheticism of the late nineteenth century, Naturalism did make an attempt to bridge the gap between life and art. Last but by no means least in this trial balance-sheet, let us not forget that Naturalism produced much vigorous, powerful writing, a good many eminently competent novels and effective plays and some that may justly rank among the world's great works of art.

Bibliography

PRIMARY SOURCES

(a) *Theoretical writings*

BECKER, G. J., *Documents of Modern Literary Realism*, Princeton, 1963.
A useful anthology of primary and secondary material about Realism and Naturalism. Extensive but occasionally inaccurate bibliography.

BAHR, H., *Die Überwindung des Naturalismus*, 1891. Reprinted Stuttgart, 1968.

HOLZ, A., *Die Kunst: ihr Wesen und ihre Gesetze*, 1890.

HUYSMANS, J.-K., *Emile Zola et 'L'Assommoir.'* Originally appeared in the journal *L'Actualité*, Brussels, 1876; reprinted in *Oeuvres Complètes*, Crès et Cie., Paris, n.d., pp. 149–92.

LINDEN, W. (editor), *Naturalismus*, Leipzig, 1936. In the series *Deutsche Literatur in Entwicklungsreihen*.
Useful excerpts from the theoretical and creative works of the German Naturalists, but the introduction is highly tendentious.

MORRISON, A., 'What is a Realist?', *New Review*, March 1897. Preface to *A Child of the Jago*, London, 1896.

RUPRECHT, E. (editor), *Literarische Manifeste des deutschen Naturalismus 1880–1892*, Stuttgart, 1962.
An excellent anthology.

TAINE, H., Introduction to *Histoire de la littérature anglaise*, Paris, 1877.

TAINE, H., Prefaces to the first and second editions of *Essais de critique et d'histoire*, 1865 and 1866.

TAINE, H., 'Balzac' in *Nouveaux essais de critique et d'histoire*, 1880.
ZOLA, E., Preface to second edition of *Thérèse Raquin*, 1867.
ZOLA, E., *Le Roman expérimental*, 1880.
ZOLA, E., *Le Naturalisme au théâtre*, 1881.
ZOLA, E., *Les Romanciers naturalistes*, 1881.
Sometimes these latter two works are reprinted in a volume under the general title *Le Roman expérimental*.

(*b*) *The Novel*

BENNETT, A., *Clayhanger*, 1910.
CRANE, S., *Maggie, Girl of the Streets*, 1893.
DREISER, T., *The Financier*, 1912.
DREISER, T., *An American Tragedy*, 1925.
FONTANE, T., *Effi Briest*, 1895.
HOLZ, A., and SCHLAF, J., *Papa Hamlet*, 1889.
Reprinted in Linden's *Naturalismus*.
MANN, T., *Buddenbrooks*, 1901.
MOORE, G., *A Mummer's Wife*, 1884.
MOORE, G., *Esther Waters*, 1893.
MORRISON, A., *A Child of the Jago*, 1896.
NORRIS, F., *McTeague*, 1899.
NORRIS, F., *Vandover and the Brute*, 1914, written 1905.
STEINBECK, J., *Tortilla Flat*, 1935.
STEINBECK, J., *The Grapes of Wrath*, 1939.
STEINBECK, J., *Cannery Row*, 1944.
ZOLA, E., *Thérèse Raquin*, 1867.
ZOLA, E., *Les Rougon-Macquart*, 1871–93.
For detailed list of *Rougon-Macquart* series see p. 45.

(*c*) *Drama*

BECQUE, H., *Les Corbeaux*, 1882 (written 1873).

BIBLIOGRAPHY 75

BRIEUX, E., *Les trois filles de M. Dupont*, 1897; *Les Avariés*, 1901; *Maternité*, 1903.
GALSWORTHY, J., *Strife*, 1909.
GORKY, M., *The Lower Depths*, 1902.
HAUPTMANN, G., *Vor Sonnenaufgang*, 1889; *Das Friedensfest*, 1890; *Einsame Menschen*, 1891; *Die Weber*, 1892; *Fuhrmann Henschel*, 1898; *Rose Bernd*, 1903; *Die Ratten*, 1911.
HOLZ, A., and SCHLAF, J., *Die Familie Selicke*, 1890.
IBSEN, H., *Pillars of Society*, 1877; *A Doll's House*, 1879; *Ghosts*, 1881; *An Enemy of the People*, 1882; *The Wild Duck*, 1884; *Rosmersholm*, 1886.
LAWRENCE, D. H., *A Collier's Friday Night*, c. 1909; *The Daughter-in-Law*, 1912; *The Widowing of Mrs Holroyd*, 1914.
OSTROVSKY, A. N., *The Storm*, 1860.
SCHLAF, J., *Meister Oelze*, 1892.
SHAW, G. B., *Plays Unpleasant*, 1898.
SUDERMANN, H., *Heimat*, 1893.
TOLSTOY, L. N., *The Power of Darkness*, 1886.

SECONDARY SOURCES

BLOCK, H. M., *Naturalistic Triptych. The Fictive and the Real in Zola, Mann and Dreiser*, New York, 1970.
A stimulating discussion of the Naturalist novel opening out of analyses of *L'Assommoir*, *Buddenbrooks* and *An American Tragedy*.
BOWRON, B. R., jun., 'Realism in America', *Comparative Literature* III, no. 3, summer 1951, pp. 268–82.
Covers Naturalism as well as Realism.
BORNECQUE, J. H., and COGNY, P., *Réalisme et Naturalisme*, Hachette, Paris, 1958; in the series 'Documents de France'.
Gives a good deal of factual information.

BRUNETIÈRE, F., *Le Roman naturaliste*, Paris, 1902.
The 'classical' work on the subject; now a curiosity of moralistic literary criticism.

CHARLTON, D. G., *Positivist Thought in France 1852–1870*, Oxford, 1959.
Assesses importance of Comte.

COGNY, P., *Le Naturalisme*, Paris 1968; in the series 'Que sais-je?'.
A sound introduction to French Naturalism.

CRUICKSHANK, J., (editor), *French Literature and its Background*, no. 5, *The Late Nineteenth Century*, Oxford, 1969.

DECKER, C. R., 'Zola's literary reputation in England', *PMLA*, xlix (1934), pp. 1140–53.
Interesting data on the reception of Zola's works in England.

FRIERSON, W. C., 'The English controversy over Realism in fiction 1885–1895', *PMLA*, xliii (1928), pp. 533–50.
A complement to Decker's article.

GOSSE, E., 'The Limits of Realism in Fiction', *Forum*, ix (June 1890) pp. 391–400. Reprinted in *Questions at Issue*, London, 1893, and in Becker, *Documents of Modern Literary Realism*, Princeton, 1963, pp. 383–93.
An indispensable essay that raises fundamental questions.

GRANT, E. M., *Emile Zola*, New York, 1966; in the series Twayne's World Authors.

HAMANN, R., and HERMAND, J., *Naturalismus*, Berlin 1968.
An invaluable survey especially of German Naturalism, interrelating literature, art, and sociology, with interesting illustrations.

HEMMINGS, F. W. J., *Emile Zola*, Oxford, 1966.
Together with Grant's book the best introduction to Zola in English; both are informative, judicious and perceptive.

HOEFERT, S., *Das Drama des Naturalismus*, Stuttgart, 1968; Sammlung Metzler no. 75.
A fully documented survey of Naturalist drama in Germany.

MARTINO, P., *Le Naturalisme français*, Paris, 1969; Collection U2.
A new version of an established work.

MÜNCHOW, U., *Deutscher Naturalismus*, Berlin, 1968; Sammlung Akademie Verlag, 1. Literatur.
To be read with discretion because of its political commitment.

RAIMOND, M., *Le Roman depuis la Révolution*, Paris, 1967; Collection U2.
Contains excellent chronological tables.

ROOT, W. H., *German Criticism of Zola, 1875–1893*, New York, 1931.
Does for Germany what Decker's article does for England.

SALVAN, A. J., *Zola aux États-Unis*, Providence, R.I., 1943.
Documents the reception of Zola in the U.S.A.

SLONIM, M., *Russian Literature from the Empire to the Soviets*, London, 1963.

STROMBERG, R. N. (editor), *Realism, Naturalism and Symbolism*, London, 1968; in the series 'Documentary History of Western Civilization'.
A collection of excerpts including some pieces otherwise hard to find.

WILLIAMS, R., *Drama from Ibsen to Eliot*, London, 1952.

Index

Alexis, Paul, 9, 27, 31, 53
Anderson, Sherwood, 35
Antoine, André, 58
Anzengruber, Ludwig, 65
Armeleutepoesie, 50

Balzac, Honoré de, 21, 25, 42
Becque, Henry, 63
Bennett, Arnold, 12, 54
Bernard, Claude, 21, 29
Bleibtreu, Karl, 37
Bölsche, Wilhelm, 13, 37
Brahm, Otto, 57
Brieux, Eugène, 59, 61, 62, 63
Brunetière, F., 6, 29, 47
Büchner, Georg, 64, 65
Céard, Henry, 27, 53
Chekhov, Anton, 61, 66
Comte, Auguste, 19, 20, 33, 34
  (*see* Positivism)
Conrad, Michael Georg, 38
Crackanthorpe, Hubert, 32
Crane, Stephen, 34, 35, 50, 54
Curel, François de, 60, 61
Cuvier, Georges, 4

Darwin, Charles, 15–16, 17, 20, 34, 42
Dickens, Charles, 6, 32, 42
Dostoievsky, Feodor, 38, 42
Dreiser, Theodore, 12, 34, 35, 51, 52

'Egerton', 32
Eliot, George, 6, 32, 42

Farrell, James T., 35
Flaubert, Gustave, 6, 25, 31, 33, 42
Fontane, Theodor, 48
Freie Bühne, 58, 63, 64

Galsworthy, John, 68
Garland, Hamlin, 7, 35
Gaskell, Mrs Elizabeth, 32, 42
Ghosts, 57, 58, 59, 60, 64
Gissing, George, 32, 50
Goncourt, Edmond & Jules, 13, 26
Gorky, Maxim, 56, 61
Grabbe, Christian Dietrich, 64

Grein, Jack, 58
Groupe de Médan, Le, 27

Harland, Henry, 32
Hauptmann, Gerhart, 12, 16, 24, 37, 38, 41, 59, 61, 64–7, 69
Hennique, Léon, 27
Hillebrand, Julius, 64
Holbach, P.H.d', 2
Holz, Arno, 37, 38, 39–40, 41, 48, 50, 67 (*see Papa Hamlet*)
Huret, Jules, 26, 31
Huysmans, Joris-Karl, 6, 24, 25, 27, 28, 31, 53

Ibsen, Henrik, 38, 40, 57, 58, 59, 60, 61, 62, 64 (*see also Ghosts*)
Impressionists, 5, 6, 26, 33
Independent Theatre of London, 58

Konsequenter Naturalismus, 40, 67

Lamarck, J.-B., 4, 15, 19
Lawrence, D. H., 68, 69
Lewis, Sinclair, 35
London, Jack, 35
Lucas, Prosper, 17

Manifeste des Cinq, 31
Mann, Thomas, 51

Marx, Karl, 22, 23, 34
Materialism, 2, 3, 12–14, 22
Maugham, W. Somerset, 50
Maupassant, Guy de, 24, 27, 31
Milieuschilderung, 66
Mill, John Stuart, 13
Moore, George, 13, 24, 30, 32, 33, 50, 54
Morrison, Arthur, 7, 32, 50
Moscow Art Theatre, 58

Norris, Frank, 12, 16, 35, 36, 51, 53

O'Casey, Sean, 68
Ostrovsky, Alexander, 55, 56

Papa Hamlet, 48–50, 52
pièce à thèse (problem play), 57, 60, 62, 68
Pisemsky, Alexey, 55, 56
Positivism, 19, 33 (*see* Comte, A.)

Renan, Ernest, 20
Roman expérimental, Le, 21, 28, 29–30, 31 (fn.)
Romantic, 1, 3, 6, 7, 8, 12, 13, 22, 24, 27, 32, 41, 51
Rougon-Macquart, Les, 17, 29, 45–6, 53, 67

Schlaf, Johannes, 48, 50, 67, (*see Papa Hamlet*)

Sekundstil, 40, 48, 52, 67
Shaw, George Bernard, 57, 59, 61, 67, 68
Sinclair, Upton, 35
Socialist realism, 66
Spencer, Herbert, 19–20, 33, 34
Steinbeck, John, 24, 34, 35, 50, 54
Stendhal, 21, 25, 42
Strindberg, August, 38, 40, 59, 61, 68
Sturm und Drang (Storm and Stress) 39, 64,
Sudermann, Hermann, 38, 67
Synge, John Millington, 68

Taine, Hippolyte, 17–18, 20–1, 25, 42

Théâtre libre, 58, 60
Thérèse Raquin, 4, 24, 28–9, 43–5, 46, 50, 53, 55, 58
Tolstoy, Leo, 6, 38, 42, 56

Useful play, 62

Verga, Giovanni, 50
Veritism, 7

Wedmore, Frederick, 32, 53
well-made play, 55, 58
Whiteing, Richard, 32

Zola, Émile, 4, 5, 6, 9, 12, 13, 16, 17, 21, 24, 25, 26–31, 33, 34–5, 38, 40, 43–6, 50, 51, 54, 55, 56, 58, 61, 63, 67

For Product Safety Concerns and Information please contact our EU representative GPSR@taylorandfrancis.com
Taylor & Francis Verlag GmbH, Kaufingerstraße 24, 80331 München, Germany

www.ingramcontent.com/pod-product-compliance
Lightning Source LLC
Chambersburg PA
CBHW052135300426
44116CB00010B/1907